Anti-Gay

To tolerate life remains, after all, the first duty of all living beings. Illusion becomes valueless if it makes this harder for us.

Sigmund Freud, *Thoughts for the Times on War and Death*
(Penguin Freud Library Vol. XII)

With best wishes
to all the LGCM
counselling helpliners.

21/1/97.   Roy Parr

Anti-Gay

Edited by Mark Simpson

FREEDOM
EDITIONS

Freedom Editions,
an imprint of the Cassell Group,
Wellington House
125 Strand
London WC2R 0BB

127 West 24th Street
New York, NY 10011

First published 1996

British Library Cataloguing-in-Publication Data
A catalogue record for this book is available from the British Library.

ISBN 0-304-33144-9 (hardback)

Typeset by Ben Cracknell Studios
Printed and bound in Great Britain by Biddles Ltd, of Guildford and
King's Lynn.

CONTENTS

ABOUT THE CONTRIBUTORS

Glenn or Glennda Belverio is a drag queen terrorist, bitchy journalist and porn model. His show *Glennda Orgasm and Friends* first aired in June 1990 and is to blame for starting the New York drag queen cable TV movement. His film *Glennda and Camille Go Downtown* with Camille Paglia was banned in New York and San Francisco and caused minor riots elsewhere. Or so he'd like to think.

Anne-Marie Le Blé is a photographer and Suzanne Patterson is a practising artist; they both live in North London. Their favourite record is *Sorry I'm a Lady* by Baccara.

Bruce LaBruce is responsible for such movies as *No Skin Off My Ass*, *Super 8½* and *Homocidal*. He was born on the exact day of Judy Garland's death and believes himself to be the reincarnation of the late legend. Even if he is Canadian.

Paul Burston is the author of *What Are You Looking At?* (Cassell, 1995), and gay section editor on *Time Out* magazine. He has been praised by the *Independent* as 'the bright bad boy of gay culture' and castigated by the editor of *Gay Times* as 'making a career out of saying the unsayable'. He isn't sure which is the greater compliment.

Jo Eadie is a writer, community worker and activist, currently wrestling with a PhD (University of Nottingham) on David Cronenberg and William Burroughs. When out of the grasp of bisexual theory he puts his time into being a parent, and worrying about whether to go on Prozac. For anyone interested in ongoing discussions about bisexuality, he can be e-mailed at 100523.2521@compuserve.com.

Toby Manning is a Manchester-based journalist whose work has appeared in the *Pink Paper*, *Gay Times*, *Attitude*, *New Statesman and Society*, the *Guardian* and the *Independent*. He isn't above biting the gay hand that used to feed him.

Lisa Power is the author of *No Bath But Plenty of Bubbles* an oral history of the London GLF 1970–73 (Cassell, 1995) and has been an activist in the gay movement for entirely too long. If she gave you a credit list of organizations you would try to fit them to her article. So let's just say that, like Mae West, she's been things and seen places.

Peter Tatchell is an activist in the queer direct action group OutRage! His recent books include *Safer Sexy – The Guide to Gay Sex Safely* (Freedom Editions, 1994) and *We Don't Want to March Straight – Masculinity, Queers and the Military* (Cassell, 1995). He is happy to work towards his own extinction.

John Weir is a novelist and journalist writing for *Details* magazine. He lives in New York. He isn't gay any more; he can't afford the gym membership (he spends too much money on phone sex).

ABOUT THE EDITOR

Mark Simpson is the author of *Male Impersonators* (Cassell, 1994) and *It's a Queer World* (Vintage, 1996). He is not a happy homosexual.

ACKNOWLEDGEMENTS

Special thanks to Nick Haeffner, fellow miserablist, whose denial of his essential gayness and clearly pathological interest in ideas and seriousness has provided much inspiration and without whom this celebratory project would not have been possible. And to Paul Burston, for being a friend, a competitor and someone who manages to be both anti-gay and too gay even for the gayest gays to stomach all at the same time, damn him.

Thanks also to *Details* magazine for giving permission to reproduce John Weir's articles 'Going In' and 'Is There Life After Sex?' (both published in 1995), and to my publisher Steve Cook at Cassell for his patience in seeing this project through to fruition.

PREFACE

Wanting to be defined by our sexuality may only be symptomatic of
our wanting to be defined. . . sexuality is what makes identity both
necessary and impossible. Because we get lost in it, we want to know
where we are.

—*Adam Philips* [1]

What is this thing call 'gay'? And is it any good?

Whatever it is, there is certainly no shortage of it. We now have
gay bars, gay priests, gay television, gay football, gay radio, gay
plagues, gay brains, gay beer, gay lifestyles, gay serial killers, gay
videos, gay counselling, gay Members of Parliament, gay magazines, gay bookshops, gay plumbers, gay pop stars, gay holidays,
gay plays, gay youths, gay ads, gay novels, gay clubs, gay condoms,
gay studies, gay soldiers, gay professionals, gay districts, gay
boutiques, gay flags, gay haircuts, gay cities, gay money, and, of
course, a gay press where all these gay things, and many more
besides, are enthusiastically profiled, interviewed, promoted and . . .
listed.

Never mind the quality, just feel the length of our lovely lists. In
1995 the most famous British gay publication, *Gay Times*, brought
out its celebratory 200th issue, billed as devoting itself to 'an
appreciation of the work and achievements of Britain's top two
hundred gay men and lesbians'. In the back was the usual 'Gay
Guide to Britain': a list of all the gay clubs, pubs and organizations
in the United Kingdom. Before that, the regular personal columns:

lists of gay people looking for other gay people, along with the regular classified lists of gay escorts, masseurs and electricians looking for gay clients. In effect the triumphant 200th edition of *Gay Times* seemed to acknowledge that the gay press could be replaced by a decent Gay Yellow Pages and that gays, whoever and whatever they are (and let's not go into that), are more obsessed with lists than Seventh Day Adventists.

This gay listing was repeated in the same year on *Gaytime TV*, the BBC's first gay TV series, this time as open farce. In a doomed attempt to introduce some face-saving irony at the start of the show the presenters demonstrated gay-marketed items such as shower curtains and aftershave in a gently mocking fashion – 'Oooh, yes, that's *very* gay' – as if to say, 'How silly! How can you have a gay shower curtain?'. But the joke rebounded on the show itself, and indeed the whole 'gay' world, since the only criterion for anything being on the show, whether it was Harvey Fierstein or the Gay Ballroom Dancing Group, was because it presented itself as 'gay'. It rapidly became apparent that the 'gayness' of shower curtains and aftershave was as legitimate a reason for attention, interest and applause as the 'gayness' of Harvey Fierstein singing a sentimental song about AIDS out of key. The whole philosophy of the show was summed up in the highly discriminating and critical attitude: 'Here's something gay. And now for something else gay'. This reached bathetic depths in the form of a regular slot called 'Camp Countdown', in which the top ten 'camp' people of that week, such as Shirley Bassey or Joan Collins, were listed in ascending order of campness – i.e. they're not gay *themselves*, but because they're 'camp' we can add them to the list of 'things-that-are-gay' under the sub-heading 'things-*for*-gays'.

So it was entirely fitting that it was another BBC TV show, *The Day Today*, a satirical comedy programme which was not gay at all and thus with a better understanding of camp than *Gaytime TV* could ever hope to have, which summed up the whole gay listing impulse in a surreal sketch where a news presenter announced, as if reporting on traffic conditions: 'Gay news now. Today large parts of Norwich will be gay, as will be the whole of the M4 and much of the Channel Islands. There is a slight chance of gayness on the western side of the Pennines'.

But life turned out to be even more surreal than Pythonesque comedy, as gay listing was taken to the molecular level. The real TV news was full of reports of claims by US scientists to have found a 'gay gene'. Gay listers rejoiced: at last there was something to put under 'G' in the Great Gay List between 'Gay Games' and 'Gay Girls'. Even more welcome was the fact that the gay gene is the first entry which justifies all the others. It is, by definition, a first principle – it doesn't need to explain itself: its existence explains everything else. And since the whole point of the Great Gay List is to avoid serious enquiry into origins or meanings, of sexuality, of language, of value, the gay gene, the origin of all gayness, if it didn't/doesn't exist would be necessary to invent.

And yet, and yet, the Great Gay List is, it must be admitted its own answer to the question: What is gay? For all its vacuity, its exhaustive not to say tedious roll call of things-that-are-gay conveys one message loud and clear – that gay is a self-serving project of self-justification. Is it any good? Well, forget that – gay *has* to be good. And this is also why it has to be named so often, not just because it fulfils the imperialist inner logic of gay (thin ideas always need to spread themselves as far and wide as possible in the hope that you won't notice their lack of substance) but also in order that a sceptical world might be convinced of gay's goodness and be forced to accept that gay is as indispensable, ubiquitous and downright lovable as the air we breathe.

This 'celebration' of homosexuality is inextricably bound up with its listy origins as Michel Foucault's famous 'reverse discourse'. In an oft-quoted but little heard passage in the introduction to his *History of Sexuality*, he describes how in the late nineteenth century, after the discovery and categorization of 'perversions' by emergent sexual and psychological sciences, 'homosexuality began to speak on its own behalf, to demand its legitimacy or "naturality" be acknowledged, often in the same vocabulary, using the same categories by which it was medically disqualified'. The lists that were used to illuminate and pathologize illegitimate ways of being became, in the hands of homosexuals themselves, an advertisement of legitimacy. Look how real, numerous and immutable we are; look how real, numerous and immutable our desires are.

And how marketable. Nowadays, gay is *goods*. The listing impulse has nicely evolved into the material function of the gay press which is to advertise gay goods, services and performers. Complaints about poor quality of these goods are redundant – the act of discrimination and approval is in the naming of them as gay in the first place. Critical faculties must be suspended once the naming moment is over (except in terms of 'how gay' – i.e. how useful to the self-justificatory project of gay). The reverse discourse has gone from political project to marketing strategy. The Great Gay (Shopping) List *is* the 'gay community'.

Well, here's something that *isn't* gay. Something that isn't straight, either, but is – heaven forfend – *Anti-Gay*.

And perhaps, given the nature of the reverse discourse, raining on gay's parade – is the only way to answer the question 'What is this thing called "gay"?', without ending up mouthing the banal and meaningless platitude 'It's good'. So contributors dwell on problems of the gay identity and lifestyle that don't exactly 'celebrate' it: the stunning vanity and arrogance of the gay world (John Weir); the intensely ambivalent attitude of gays towards bisexuals, wanting to swallow them whole but nearly choking in the process (Jo Eadie); the mindless mediocrity of gay culture (Toby Manning);

the way lesbians build their own prison out of buzz-cuts, big boots and a general contempt for femininity (Anne-Marie Le Blé and Suzanne Patterson); the befuddled arguments censorious gay critics employ in dubbing films like *Cruising* 'homophobic' (Paul Burston); and the uncomfortable 'truth' of Camille Paglia's reminder that 'penis fits vagina' and the corresponding benefits of being cured of one's homosexuality (Bruce LaBruce and Glenn Belverio).

However anti-gay the contributors to this volume may or may not be themselves (and Lisa Power and Peter Tatchell, both veterans of the Gay Liberation Front era make here a critical case *for* gay), clearly they all have problems with the feel-good-or-else politics that is associated with gay. Indeed, sometimes you might be forgiven for thinking that being gay is like being made to wear that electronic helmet designed by tongue-lolling cheery Stimpy for his misanthropic friend Ren which forces the wearer to grin inanely and sing the 'Happy, Happy, Joy, Joy' song.

That many non-heterosexuals were already itching to escape from gay's clingy, cartoony embrace has already been demonstrated with queer. Perhaps the less said about this moment the better. But there was initially at least a strong strain of punkish transgression running through queer which was quite liberating for many. Groups like Homocult, the situationist art collective in Manchester, who specialized in 'negative' images of homosexuality; North American zinesters like *Bimbox* who arguably invented queer; the work of film directors like Bruce LaBruce, Tom Kalin, and Todd Haynes who, as Kalin put it, aimed to put the 'homo' back in 'homicide'; and Queercore, a bad-attitude thrash sound attracting a younger generation of deviants who didn't want or weren't wanted by what they took to be heterosexuality but didn't want to sip cappuccino on Old Compton Street or Santa Monica Boulevard either.[2]

And while these cultural manifestations of queer are far from being played out (see Toby Manning's contribution), like the punk that it took its inspiration from it was an avant-gardism that was assimilated by the mainstream almost immediately. But, ironically, the 'straight' mainstream seems to have been changed more by this assimilation than the gay mainstream. The straight mainstream got the New Queer Cinema and Madonna's *Sex*; the gay mainstream got Michelangelo Signorile and 'QUEER AS FUCK' T-shirts.

Gay, in short, did with queer precisely what it always lambasted the 'straight world' for doing: it took what it wanted and disregarded and suppressed the threatening stuff. The gay press preferred to overlook the anti-gay side to queer and dwelled instead on queer's attack on heterosexism and homophobia in the form of the ACT UP style zaps of groups like OutRage! and Queer Nation. Queer's problem was not that it was assimilated by straights so much as it was assimilated by *gays*. It became, as Paul Burston put it, 'Gay with knobs and nipple rings'. Gay politics, in its queer get-up, *was* badly-behaved and, in that now cringe-making phrase, 'in-yer-face' – but only in the face of heterosexuals.

However, in the academic world – which, after all, at least has to pretend to a critical approach – the advance of what has been called queer theory, with its deconstruction of sexual and gender identities exemplified in the work of Judith Butler and Eve Kosofsky Sedgwick (heavily influenced by the work of the three French post-structuralist stooges, Derrida, Lacan and Foucault) has already upset gay apple carts and worried some of the gay old timers that used to hawk from them.

According to the (for once with good cause) celebrated gay critic Leo Bersani, 'gay men and lesbians have nearly disappeared into their awareness of how they have been *constructed* as gay men and lesbians . . . having de-gayed themselves, gays melt into the culture they like to think of themselves as undermining'.[3] Anyone who has walked through Soho or attended Gay Pride recently might be forgiven for laughing at the idea that gays are disappearing into their own awareness of how they have been constructed. But Bersani is really talking about gay intellectuals. And perhaps he has a point when he writes that 'the power of these systems [that have created the category of the homosexual] is only minimally contested by demonstrations of their "merely" historical character. They don't need to be natural to rule . . . '. Undoubtedly, a lot of queer theory is little more than linguistic or historical pedantry that is far more irritating than it is 'challenging'.

Surely, however, 'de-gaying' oneself is not something that you embark upon because you think that it will Change the World, but because, as in the course of a feud that you've quite enjoyed up until now, or at least felt self-righteous about, you suddenly discover that you're very bored and don't want to go on playing Tweedle Dum to someone else's Tweedle Dee forever. 'De-gaying' is also the inevitable result of postmodernism finally catching up with gay and fragmenting its pretentious 'grand-narrative'. People are leaving gay because they no longer believe its claims to interpret the world or make it a better place.

As others have pointed out, the gay *v.* straight binary is a *cul de sac* without any turning space; continuing to subscribe to it, even critically in Bersani fashion, is like insisting on pretending that 'left-wing' and 'right-wing' still have a solid meaning post-1980s, when the most radical programmes began to come from right-wing parties. Even Camille Paglia, arch-opponent of post-structuralism and queer theory 'flim-flammery', and dubbed 'essentialist' by many of her flim-flamming critics, argues for a 'bisexual responsiveness' in all, that human sexuality should be regarded as fluid rather than fixed, and calls for gay studies, along with women's studies, to be abolished and replaced with sex studies.[4]

But Bersani and many gays of his generation, just like the older feminists excoriated by Paglia and happy to excoriate her back, appear to want the younger generation to fight over again the battles of their youth, regardless of whether they need fighting again. Just as there is and can be no such thing as 'post-feminism', there is no 'post-gayism' – there is only letting the side down or collaboration. This is apparent in Bersani's circular argument that 'de-gaying gayness can only fortify homophobic oppression; it accomplishes in its own way the principal aim of homophobia: the elimination of gays'.[5] But if we shouldn't de-gay ourselves because it's what homophobia wants, it follows that it is our duty to be defined by homophobia. This, to my mind, really doesn't read any different to: we have to be gay because homophobia *wants* us to be. And in fact it is evident from Bersani's own argument that gay needs homophobia just as much as homophobia needs gay. After all, this wouldn't be the first time in history that a system which was supposed to revolutionize human relations ended up being concerned only with its own survival.

To be fair, Bersani is that rare species, a gayist who himself recognizes some of the failings of gay. He confesses that there is 'little self-criticism within the gay and lesbian community'[6] and that 'straight oppression' is not enough of an excuse for this behaviour any more: 'We have enough freedom, even enough power, to stop feeling like traitors if we cease to betray our intelligence for the sake of the cause, and if . . . we admit to have told a few lies about ourselves (and others)'.[7] But in the context of his broader plea for continuing to rally to the party and for a little more discipline in the 'melting' ranks, his appeal for *glasnost* seems to be a case of too little too late and anyway, only likely to accelerate the break-up of gay. As the Communist Party of the Soviet Union found out, if in the name of a new openness you deprive people of their reassuring myths, what are they left with? Just a lot of barbed wire and shoddy goods.

Chastened by the failure of queer's grandiose ambitions, this collection of malodorous essays by various disgruntled non-heterosexuals does not pretend to offer a new manifesto or movement that puts the Children of Sodom back on course for the Promised Land. It doesn't even pretend to be much more 'inclusive' than gay (only two contributions by women, only one bisexual and none from people of colour). Actually, it doesn't promise anything other than the merciless operation of critical faculties where gay demands they be suspended, censored or diverted into 'fighting homophobia'.

And, who knows? By focusing on the shortcomings of gay and refusing to be distracted by how terrible heterosexuality is supposed to be, *Anti-Gay* may even offer the beginnings of a new dialectic, a new conversation with the world, one that is rather more interesting than the current one. Perhaps, just perhaps, the anti-thesis contained within *Anti-Gay* might one day produce a synthesis that will replace the awful gay thesis that we appear to be trapped in right now. And put and end to those damn lists.

Notes

1. Adam Phillips, *Terrors and Experts* (London: Faber, 1995), p. 90.
2. Caroline Sullivan, 'Queer to the Core', *Guardian*, 17 December 1993.
3. Leo Bersani, *Homos* (Cambridge: Harvard University Press, 1995), p. 6.
4. Camille Paglia, *Vamps and Tramps* (London: Viking, 1995), p. 121.
5. Bersani, *Homos,* p. 5.
6. Bersani, *Homos*, p. 52.
7. Bersani, *Homos*, p. 55.

Anti-Gay

Chapter One

GAY DREAM BELIEVER:
INSIDE THE GAY UNDERWEAR CULT
Mark Simpson

I hope that now you're Out, life improves for you no end. You've lifted the burden of secrecy and deceit and that might mean that the other problems that have plagued you will simply evaporate.

—*Gay Times* columnist *Terry Sanderson* in an open letter in the *Guardian* to the entertainer Michael Barrymore

I wanna be free, gay and happy!

—*The Coming Out Crew*

I am a homosexual in a city full of gays.

—*Michel Foucault* in San Francisco

Isn't it just fabby to be gay? Gay is, after all, good, and everyone fortunate enough to be gay is, of course, glad – when they're not too busy feeling proud. Which is perfectly understandable since gays, as we all know, have the best clubs, the best drugs, the best underwear shops and the best time. In fact, gays are so glad and proud that they have a big, sweaty street party every year to show the world just how glad and proud they are and what great underwear they have.

All things considered, it's so fabby being gay, that it's difficult to imagine what it must be like to be straight. Imagine the suffering of those poor souls who are doomed by some accident of genetics or underdevelopment of that brain lobe which regulates aesthetic potential not only to never be able really to appreciate *Ab Fab* or carry off wearing a silver thong but also never to be able to come out. Imagine never being able to experience the joy of discovering your true identity and inheriting all this gladness; imagine being excluded from a world so marvellous, so welcoming, so well-presented, simply because you thought having children and living in the suburbs seemed like the thing to do.

Even worse, imagine what it would be like actually to prefer the same sex but be denied the rewards that this display of good taste so rightly entails and be forced to pass for straight. Difficult as it is to believe, this was once the universal state of affairs. This is because – horrible to relate – once upon a time there were no gays only dreary *homosexuals*.

Naturally, this was before that watershed moment in human history by which everything must be measured – the Stonewall Revolution. Before Stonewall, or BS, homosexuals had internalized straight values and were labouring under oppression and a false sense of guilt. They thought themselves ill or sinful or both. So, in dimly-lit, underworld-controlled basement bars, wearing cardigans in muted colours, they cried into their Martinis and looked enviously at the carefree drag queens – so strong, so colourful, so successful with straight trade. As disco had not been invented yet – there being no gays to sniff poppers and whoop it up in bell-bottoms – the pitiful homosexuals' only solace was singing along to Judy Garland's 'The Man That Got Away' and, of course, 'Over the Rainbow'.

No wonder these poor creatures would often be heard lamenting their lot, expressing shame and wishing out loud that they could be cured of their sad affliction.

However, in 1969 at the Stonewall Inn in Greenwich Village, New York, all this changed. Forever. During the course of another police raid by heartless pigs unconcerned that the homos had buried poor Judy's bones only the day before, something unheard of happened. Inspired to anger by the drag queens' feisty show of resistance, the

2

homos revolted. An ear-ring or beer bottle brutally ripped from some fierce, befrocked lovely resisting arrest, crashed to the floor and the *ancien regime* of homo-shame shattered into a thousand dangerous pieces as the rioting that changed the world began.

Exhilarated by their new-found Gay Power the rioters had a revelation. It dawned on them that their sense of guilt and shame was just a trick designed to keep them out of sight and in conservative clothes. There was no longer any need to repress their desires or their undergarments, or acquiesce in the New York Police Department's attempt to repress *them*.

Armed with the new-found weapon of Gay Pride they fought back, surprising and vanquishing the entire NYPD whose Irish muscle, used to yielding fag flesh, now found itself impotent against the righteous anger of these empowered pansies. That magical night all the homosexuals in New York became gay and flooded out of their basement bars, darkened piers and parks, onto the streets, peeling off their sweaters, discarding their corduroy trousers and shouting out the message for all the world to hear: Gay is Good! The cure for their sad affliction had turned out to be not prayer, psychiatry, electro-shock or football but Gay Pride.

That message resounded around the world. After Stonewall, or AS, homos everywhere began to discover the indisputable truth that gay is as moral, as natural, as healthy, as beautiful as they had been told homosexuality was immoral, unnatural, unhealthy and ugly. The Stonewall Revolution corrected society's misconception about homosexuality not by turning the world upside down but by turning it the right way up: the inverts merely overturned a world that was already standing on its head.

So, in the AS epoch, homosexuality, with its nasty medicinal odour, was now an increasingly redundant term. Instead, 'homophobia', a word with a nasty medicinal odour, was coined to explain the origins of the obviously mentally imbalanced idea that gay wasn't good. While the innocent BS homosexual was the victim of pathologization and prejudice, the guilty AS homophobe was obviously *deserving* of pathologization and prejudice. It soon became apparent that since homophobia was an illness produced by ignorance, secrecy, and an aversion to wearing leather harnesses in public, the underlying cause of homophobia was a shortage of proud gays.

This was underlined by the fact that the homophobe was invariably a homosexual who wouldn't accept his destiny/duty and become gay. In fact, it was soon recognized that any congruence of same-shaped genitals, or interest in such congruence, however casual or passing, anywhere in the world at any time must eventually be paid for by full membership of the gay community and an account with 'Big Boy Athletic Support Supplies' or else face charges of hypocrisy and living a lie.

Gays quickly discovered another, related, truth. If gay was good – and this was an *a priori* truth – then the gay life was also the good life, in every sense. So not only was being gay a real gas, and as you know, really fabby, but it was the *moral* thing to do. Homosexuals had been encouraged to say 'no' to themselves several times a day (or at least feel guilty about not saying it). Gays, on the other hand, would learn to say 'Yes please!' several times before brunch.

In fact, square, trad old 'no' was not a word that gays had time for anymore. Once the ultimate 'no' had been shouted at Stonewall – 'No!' to a world of shame, 'No!' to straight convention, 'No!' to cotton/polyester mix jockey shorts – there was no need ever to say 'no' again. Moreover, 'to your own self be true' was the Disney-esque existential motto of gays everywhere – and since as a gay your sexuality/pleasure was you, saying 'no' to any form of indulgence was a denial of the truth of who you were. Abstinence was a form of mendacity at best and collaboration at worst – since saying 'yes' to yourself was also the gay way of continuing to say 'no' to straight convention, hedonism was a positive virtue and absolute duty. After Stonewall abolished guilt overnight where centuries of philosophizing had failed, the only thing to feel guilty about now was feeling guilty itself. This is how gays invented the 1970s and made the world safe for designer underwear.

Of course, the thrilling times of Stonewall are a long way behind us now. But their spirit is very much alive today. The life-transforming revelation and truth of Stonewall is repeated every time someone comes out and is baptized into the gay community. The truth shall still set ye free. When one comes out, and ceases to be a private homosexual and becomes instead a public gay, the burden of deceit and false consciousness is thrown off, the sex police are vanquished and the out person demonstrates new-found whistle-blowing pride in sexuality instead of shame. It is a confessional narrative of sinner and saved. When a man comes out as gay he is coming out as what he was meant to be all along – he has found his true self, his existential soul, and rejected the sin/guilt of the previous, inauthentic, closeted self that thought baggy clothes were quite comfortable really.

And now that the scales have fallen down from the new convert's eyes he is born again – not in the silly, lying, sex-negative fundamentalist sense of the word, of course, but in a new meaningful, sex-positive, *gay* sense. And indeed sense itself is bestowed upon the lucky soul who comes out. His whole hitherto confusing life has been leading up to this moment – a long gestation period spent in the chrysalis of the closet. What seemed without purpose before now takes on meaning. What's more, the other problems that have plagued him will disappear. Coming out is thus a moment of revelation and redemption: I was blind, but now I see; I was lost, but now I'm found. Just like the homos in the Stonewall Bar that night in Year Zero, from the nasty straight-acting homosexual grub emerges a fabulous gay butterfly with wings of lycra.

Coming out is also a form of death – but a fabulous life-affirming form of death to be sure. To be 'reborn' you have to destroy the wrong person that existed before. So the out person now recalls that he knew he was gay from the earliest age; before he encountered puberty, before he could walk, before the afterbirth was cold, etc., etc. Early playground friendships with members of the same sex are now seen for what they were: passionate gay attachments which no one straight could possibly have entertained. On the other hand, any encounters with, interest in or marriage to the opposite sex is now quite rightly seen as nothing but an ill-judged attempt to satisfy one's peers, parents, guilt, false consciousness or just sisterly feeling. You know the scenario: I thought I loved you, but really I just envied your make-up skills.

And best of all, the newly emerged out person also discovers that a sense of difference and apartness, feelings of aloneness and hollowness common to most at some time or other and exploited by all nasty religions – especially the anti-gay ones – are in fact a product of being homosexual but unable to become gay. It is surely a great consolation to know that the real reason for your sense of smallness and strangeness in the universe as a child was not because you were human and frail, or separated from God, but because you were meant to dance till dawn in a Spandex all-in-one, surrounded by young men with mobile hips and chemical smiles, and yet were stuck in a Gap-less town in Cleveland where the only place open after 11 pm was the deathburger van outside the Young Farmers Club.

And it has to be the case, doesn't it? If coming out isn't a coming home, then it would mean that homos were still lost souls who have to face the universe alone. And that would be a bit of a downer, really.

That sense of difference is anyway replaced by an enveloping, snuggly sense of *sameness* when you come out. In the gay world everything is reassuringly similar, wherever you go. Gays are better at franchizing than McDonalds. Just in case you should feel homesick when travelling abroad or just around town, gay bars and clubs around the globe are playing the same music and the patrons are wearing the same jeans, haircuts and even facial expressions. In the backroom the same American porn movie is showing and men are on their knees performing the same acts they see on the screen and rapping the same rap in the same Strykerese. And wherever you go you can pick up a gay publication which is full of pictures of people just like you and exciting information on just how many other people just like you there are out there and how you can meet them. Once you're out you need never be troubled by pesky old difference ever again.

An inconvenient sense of insignificance and humdrumness is also eradicated when you come out. When you come out you are midwife and mother to your own birth. Nature and heterosexuality have no claim on you anymore as you become a godlike creature of culture. By heroically refusing to allow contact between penis and vagina the gay man refuses to accept his mortality and the ignominy of driving space-mobiles (even if reproduction occurs, as a result of some drunken accident or some sober design of turkey basters).

Straights, on the other hand, are doomed to be the mere vassals of nature and Pampers shareholders. Their bodies are used in a cruel and mercenary way merely to mix genes together, to pass the new gene line on to the next generation and to pay school fees. Gays, meanwhile, use each other's bodies in a tender and beautiful way to mix together aftershaves and pass on new fashion lines to the next generation.

In this sense, gays, contrary to their perception by many straights as the embodiment of immoral 'animal lust', are actually a brand of holy celibates. Yes, some may be very promiscuous, but only with other men, a choice of partner which – until the appearance of AIDS – was a form of sexual activity with absolutely no consequences (unless you count increased expenditure on Crisco and Kleenex).

But perhaps the most marvellous thing of all about coming out is that you leave psychoanalysis behind as something for uptight straights. When a man makes the transition from homosexual to gay, he is choosing light over dark, truth over falsehood, reason over superstition, rationality over convention, expression over repression, Calvin Klein over Hanes; he is emerging from the twilight world into the sunlit uplands of life where everyone has a great tan-line. The homosexual who walks out of his stuffy closet and into the open arms of the gay community is in fact conducting a walking cure instead of a talking cure, one which renders all further analysis, or even thought, completely redundant.

Everything is now, by definition, out in the open. The gay man knows who he is, what he is, what he wants and where to find it at a ten per cent discount. There are no longer any conflicts to be told, any mysteries to unravel or any dreams to be interpreted. Nothing needs to be unlocked because this has already been done by opening the closet door – Eros has been liberated, inhibition vanquished. After the gay man's debut on the world stage as a fully formed person with fully formed needs and fully formed pectorals, everything is exactly as it appears to be. The gay man is, in fact, the very embodiment of enlightened common sense, full rationality and great grooming. And there is absolutely no truth in the scurrilous idea put around by anti-gay people and those, like Camille Paglia, who are No Friends of the Gay Community, that this is why homosexuals were more interesting to talk to or, for that matter, read.

When you consider all the advantages of coming out, you can't help but come to the conclusion that it is a pity that it happens only once in your life.

Which is why the Pride Parade was invented. At Pride, everyone can come out year after year. And they can do this *en masse* – just like the original Stonewall rioters. Everyone has the chance to feel like they are changing the world and, even more importantly, to try and draw as much attention to themselves as possible. So on the June anniversary of Year Zero, gays in big cities parade through town, hold hands, kiss and embrace, and blow whistles, while the fetishists in their ranks display their paraphernalia, drag queens flaunt their stuff, male strippers flex and pose on floats sponsored by sexual lubricant companies, and young men in their underwear formation dance to Madonna's 'Vogue'. Everyone has the chance to noisily relive and dramatize the excitement and the liberation of their own coming out, vanquishing any counter-revolutionary thoughts they might be entertaining about the muted anticlimax that may actually have followed this curtain-raiser.

And there are many reasons to feel proud at Pride. You are proud to prefer the same sex, proud to be open about it, proud of your floats and Freedom Flags, proud to be there feeling proud and especially proud of your cycling shorts three sizes too small. It's quite dizzying, really. No wonder many people describe it as a 'near religious experience'. It's a wonder that proud gay hearts don't just burst with pride on such a proud day. The straight world can only look on in bitter frustration, realizing that in spite of their best efforts they haven't succeeded in making gays hung up about their sexuality.

As a measure of how successful and how popular gay is, every year the parades get bigger, the floats fluffier and the male strippers beefier and oilier. In case we don't notice this, the gay press helpfully points this out – along with the cast-iron prediction that this year the parade will be so big, fluffy and oily that the straights won't be able to ignore it, like they somehow managed to last year (not counting, that is, those couple of photos of drag queens whose lives and choice of heels were obviously being validated because a camera was pointing in their direction).

9

And knowing that the numbers are growing each year is gratifying news. It tells us that we are on the road to victory, that we must have right on our side, and, best of all, that we are fashionable.

But perhaps the most encouraging thing about the rising attendance figures is that they bring ever closer the realization of the greatest gay dream of all: to turn the whole world into a gay disco! After all, Pride is nothing if it isn't a vast gay day-club; a discotheque after the lights have come on but no one wants to go home.

Understandably, the Coming of the Kingdom of Kylie is something that most gays can hardly wait for. A world of free love and shirtless men with their hands in the air showing you their shaved armpits is something really to look forward to. Just think of the money saved on taxi fares for a start. And what better image could there be of freedom and love than the gay disco? With just a teensy-weensy bit of help from mind-altering substances, the gay disco is the place where you can experience the most intense sense of well-being, belonging and happiness, not to mention some really interesting conversations about life, the universe and how difficult it is to get hold of good shit these days and how the tab you took last weekend turned the whites of your eyes yellow.

But this magic is not something that gays want to keep for themselves. Gays are so unselfish, so giving and so concerned about the rest of the world that they devoutly want to extend this dry-ice Nirvana to everyone else, just so long as they're cute and under thirty-five. And by one of those strange coincidences which makes you realize that Dame Fate is actually a fag hag herself, straights under thirty-five, lured by techno, house and lycra-cotton mix underwear, are exactly the ones who are queuing up outside the gay disco wanting a piece of Utopia plus strobe lights. Everyone cool now wants to dream the gay dream, or at least stay up all night dancing to their records.

So gays, you see, really have reached the other side of the rainbow that Judy sang about it. Now that we're out of the closet and not living in Kansas or Cleveland anymore we don't need to cry into our Martinis. In fact, such behaviour is not to be tolerated at all, being as it is just a sign that you haven't really 'come to terms' yet or that you are just some terrible self-hating throwback. Any unhappiness is clearly the result of straight oppression, self-oppression or your dealer not having the right contacts.

Besides, we have everything you could ask for, and if, by some strange delusion, you feel you're missing something in your life, thoughtful niche marketeers will think of it for you. The gay press, courtesy of kind telephone sex operators and their lovely sex-positive ads featuring buffed men in some really stunning underwear, is free and never stops telling us how marvellous we and the products aimed at us are. Gay pressure groups tell us we are adorable victims who deserve special protection and sympathy, while market researchers tell us we are adorable consumers who deserve special targeting. Really big stars like Shirley Maclaine and Liza Minnelli love us. Madonna wants to be one of us. The younger generation wants to dance with us. And, God bless their bikini lines, Bob 'n' Rob Jackson Paris and their parakeets are role-modelling for us.

When all is said and done, the only thing to feel sorry about, apart, of course, from the fact that the Olympic Commission hasn't yet accepted the Wet Jockstrap Contest as a sport, is AIDS . But even then sadness isn't what you should be feeling, except during those touching candlelit vigils. Instead you should be feeling angry at drug companies/the Government/Western medicine/the CIA/straights for letting it happen and pride at the heroic way gays have responded to it and dismissing as patently homophobic and therefore not worth discussing, the suggestion that AIDS might not have been a gay plague in the West, that gays might not have had to respond to it so heroically without the ghettoism and hedonism of the gay seventies and the gay identity itself.

After having discovered at Stonewall the Truth that gay is always good and having been set free by that discovery, at last seeing and showing things as they really are, gays have indeed changed the world and the shape of men's briefs forever. No wonder we feel so proud of our achievements. Isn't it fabby to be gay?

Chapter Two

IS THERE LIFE AFTER SEX?
John Weir

It's June in San Francisco, and the weather is so fine it's like a rebuke. I'm walking through the Mission District with Elliot Ramos, an AIDS-prevention educator at a major city agency that provides services for people with AIDS. I can't mention the agency's name without getting Elliot in trouble, which is my first clue that it's impossible to discuss AIDS prevention without making people crazy. Everyone from televangelists to gay activists has a stake in setting the limits of safe sex. Consequently, Elliot's talking to me not as an AIDS professional, but as a friend. We're not friends – we've known each other for about fifteen minutes – but we might as well be. San Francisco's like that. People get close fast. As it happens, Elliot is originally from New York, but that's true of a lot of people here. San Francisco's where New Yorkers come in order not to feel ashamed of being nice.

Elliot's twenty-seven but he looks eleven, a dark-haired Christopher Robin with a goatee. He's in the risk group for AIDS that has been getting some attention lately – guys in their late teens and twenties. They're part of a so-called second wave of HIV infection, meaning that people who were in grammar school and high school in the mid-80s are now testing positive for HIV in numbers not much lower than ten years ago. Furthermore, according to recent statistics from the Centers for Disease Control and Prevention, AIDS is now the leading cause of death among everyone – men and women, straight and gay – aged twenty-five to forty-four. Anyone who thought HIV would stop being spread by the mid 1990s was being naive. I was naive. Now I'm in San Francisco to get enlightened. How is it possible that young people, who have known about the virus since high school, are still taking risks? Don't they know better? Don't they know how devastating AIDS is? Or have all the efforts to educate Americans about HIV transmission and living with and dying from AIDS simply failed?

Maybe I failed. For the past twelve years, I've been involved with groups like ACT UP and Gay Men's Health Crisis, fighting against and educating about AIDS. One of my goals was to protect people who were HIV-negative from getting infected – people like Elliot, who says he's HIV-negative, 'as far as I know'. Today is his day off, and he's dressed like a skate punk, in low-slung baggy shorts and a T-shirt, with a black canvas bag that keeps slipping off his shoulder.

At Sixteenth Street, we watch a young guy as lean and wobbly as Gumby cross Valencia. He's stained by golden sunlight so supersaturated that it looks like he's gliding through butterscotch pudding. Paradise accelerated: Elliot tells me the guy's probably tweeking. I'm too dense for the reference. 'Speeding' Elliot says, 'doing speed. Methamphetamines. Didn't you notice how many people are spinning out this morning? They're still high from last night'. Of course, he's right. It's the Friday before the annual Gay Freedom Day Parade, a big party weekend, and the city is wound tight as a frat house gearing up for Spring Riot.

I ask Elliot if he's ever tweeked, and he says, 'Yeah'. I ask him how it's usually done, whether people snort it or shoot it or what, and he says, 'Pretty much whatever way you want. Dilute it in water even and drink it'. 'Like Alka-Seltzer?' I say. 'More like Kool-Aid', he says. Then he describes in detail the advantages of shooting it up your butt with a needleless syringe. 'So if you want to get into something heavy later, like fisting', he says, 'you're not going to feel it so much'.

I ask him if he really believes that speed messes with your judgement so much that you forget to worry about AIDS. 'Figure

that you're with a guy you like', he says. 'Maybe the speed is
making your thoughts go really fast, and you're thinking, "He's hot,
this is fun, where's the condom?" You know? It's not like you don't
worry about it. It's that you worry for like a split second, and then
the speed takes the thought away and suddenly you're doing it, and
that's that'. Then I ask him point-blank if he's done that – let
someone penetrate him without a condom when he was high on
speed – and he looks at me guilelessly and simply says, 'Yes'.

That stops me. My best friend died of AIDS last October, and I'm
still in shock. A month after his death, another close friend tested HIV-
positive . He's thirty-two and he's never engaged in anything riskier
than oral sex without ejaculation. When I heard the news, I decided not
just never to have sex again, but to convince all my friends never to
have sex again. I was as crazed and angry as Jesse Helms denouncing
gay sex on the floor of the US Senate. Helms is the famously
antihomosexual Republican senator from North Carolina who says
that people get AIDS because of their 'deliberate, disgusting, revolting
conduct'. I didn't think sex was disgusting and revolting, just fatal.
Doing it without a condom struck me as lethally deliberate. If people
are having anal sex without condoms, I thought, they're getting
infected on purpose. Either that, or they truly don't know better.

Then there's Elliot, likeable and smart, telling me the truth about
HIV transmission, which, even now, I'm reluctant to believe. Elliot
educates people about HIV transmission for a living, but unlike a lot
of professional AIDS educators, he's honest about his own sexual
behaviour. It's not that he doesn't know better. He knows way better.
And he doesn't seem to have a particular desire to get HIV-infected
– he hasn't mentioned a death wish or talked about how toying with
danger is sexy. He's just telling me he was stoned and careless a
couple of times.

In other words, he's twenty-seven and feels immortal. Or, like a
lot of gay men, he has issues with self-esteem. Or he closed his eyes

15

and pretended that he was Drew Barrymore and the other guy was Chris O'Donnell, and the fantasy carried him away. Or maybe it just happened. I'm looking for ways to justify what he did, but the point is simple, and almost impossible to accept: knowing how HIV is spread will not stop people from doing the things that might spread it. It hasn't stopped Elliot, and it hasn't stopped me, and it probably won't stop you.

AIDS prevention is based on the unlikely theory that when people are told something is bad for them, they'll avoid it. Here are some statistics that prove otherwise: one in ten homosexual or bisexual men aged seventeen to twenty-two in Berkeley and in San Francisco is infected with HIV, according to a study conducted in 1992 and 1993 by the San Francisco Department of Public Health. Nearly one in five homosexual or bisexual men aged eighteen to twenty-nine in San Francisco is infected with HIV, according to a survey run in 1992 and 1993 by the University of California San Francisco Medical Center. The UCSF study shows a 2.6 per cent yearly rate of conversion from HIV-negative to HIV-infected among eighteen- to twenty-nine-year-olds, meaning that another 26 per cent of men currently in this age group will be HIV-infected in ten years. Forty out of every one hundred young men who regularly have sex with men and who live in San Francisco will be infected with HIV before their fortieth birthday. Often well before. These are conservative estimates.

San Francisco is not exceptional. While the number of reported cases of AIDS has fallen nationwide since 1993, HIV infection transmitted by men having sex with men is, after a period of decline, back on the rise. Moreover, such cases among men thirteen and older are increasing everywhere except in the Northeast, especially in the South and Midwest, and especially among African-Americans and Latinos. While newly diagnosed AIDS cases have dropped among white homosexual men, they have increased in every other ethnic group. And though new infections with HIV are down for older gay men, they are rising among younger ones. 'By the time these guys are thirty-five and forty', says Dennis Osmond, one of the authors of the UCSF study, 'between 35 and 40 per cent of them will be infected. This is not a whole lot of improvement over the previous generation'.

'Testing HIV-positive is becoming its own rite of passage in San Francisco'. I hear this on an achingly clear spring day from an instant new friend, Eric Rofes. We're sitting in a coffee shop on Castro Street, across from the Castro Street Theater, with its famous Beaux Arts marquee. The Castro District is a theme park of the gay-rights movement. Same-sex couples holding hands stroll like straight families in Disneyland, wearing their souvenir T-shirts: 'GAY AND PROUD' and 'KISS ME, I MIGHT BE A PRINCESS'. At the corner, leather daddies and butch lesbian bottoms wait together affably for the cable car.

Eric is a transplanted New Yorker, but he's almost twenty years older, as tall and shaggy and bearded as one of the Allman Brothers. When he tells me he's a graduate student at Berkeley, it's like a flashback to the 60s. But he's a refugee of the Reagan 80s, a survivor of the first generation of gay men to be affected by AIDS. 'I'm noticing a new scenario among younger guys, though', he tells me. 'You take a high-school kid, he figures out he's gay. He goes to college and experiments a little. Then at twenty-two or twenty-three he moves to San Francisco, or New York, or Boston. He goes through all the rituals: joins a gym, gets his body pierced, a tattoo, whatever. Now he's finally "gay"'. Eric pauses, smiling ruefully. 'By twenty-eight, he's infected with HIV. By thirty-four, he's got AIDS. By thirty-six, he's dead'.

Eric's talking about what some journalists and gay activists call the second wave. The second wave had its media moment recently, reported in *The New Republic* and *The New York Times* and discussed on *60 Minutes*. It was presented as a startling new development, a sudden and inexplicable rise in HIV infection, just at the point when everybody assumed no one was having unsafe sex any more. Ask people who work for AIDS-prevention agencies in San Francisco about the second wave, however, and they'll tell you it's a ruse, a non-issue, a trumped up public health phenomenon calculated to get middle-class white people worried about AIDS again.

'The rate of infection among teens and guys in their early twenties isn't new, it's just newly acknowledged', according to Eric Ciasullo, an ecstatic thirty-two-year-old San Francisco AIDS activist. Eric is HIV-positive, and so is Loras Ojeda, another intense energetic thirty-two-year-old who works with gays twenty-three and younger at San Francisco's Lyric, the Lavender Youth Recreation and Information Center. Loras puts things more bluntly. Noting the steady and unabated increase of AIDS cases among blacks and Latinos over the whole course of the epidemic, he says, 'It's all the same fucking wave, man. It's all the same *wake*'.

Kerrington Osborne, the black-clad, braceleted, and dreadlocked thirty-two-year-old executive director of the National Task Force on AIDS prevention, quotes from a sheet of paper filled with statistics about the rise in cases of AIDS among African-American men. Kerrington is scathingly intelligent, part snap diva, part Denzel Washington getting things under control in *Crimson Tide*. He's a single parent, a Harvard graduate, and a Capricorn. When I tell him I'm writing, about a new rise in HIV infection, he says, 'What's new about it?'. Then he grabs his sheet of facts and figures and rattles off the data: 'Between 1989 and 1994, diagnosed cases of AIDS among men having sex with men rose 51 per cent in the Midwest and 49 per cent in the South', he reads. 'AIDS cases rose 79 per cent among African-American men, 77 per cent among Native American men, 61 per cent among Latino men, 55 per cent among Asian and Pacific Islander men, and 14 per cent among white men'.

18

In other words, like Elliot, like Eric Rofes, like Eric Ciasullo and Loras Ojeda, and like Johnny Symons at the Stop AIDS Project, who estimates that most young gay men in San Francisco get infected with HIV within six months of moving here, Kerrington is stating the obvious: people are still getting infected, and they're still dying. You can call it a second wave if you want. The fact is, fourteen years into the epidemic – at least twelve years since doctors figured out how the AIDS virus is transmitted – people are still spreading the disease. 'Considering that there's maybe a ten- or eleven-year average span from HIV infection to being diagnosed with AIDS', Eric tells me, 'then in a couple more years it's going to be clear that everybody getting sick must have been infected after 1985, when they were supposed to "know better". What are all the Elizabeth Taylors going to say then?'.

They might say they've been reading Walt Odets and are trying to understand. Walt Whitman Odets – an impassioned middle-aged gay Berkeley psychologist – is the son of the famous 1930s leftist playwright Clifford Odets, who wrote *Awake and Sing!*. Odet's articles about AIDS prevention have the same fervent and exclamatory energy of his father's pro-union playwriting. 'The chasm between what we know [about HIV transmission] and what we tell gay men is immense and bewildering', he writes in a clinical treatise on AIDS prevention among gay men, which was reprinted in *Harper's*. According to Odets, asking all gay men to use a condom every time they have oral or anal sex is imposing a rigid, and sometimes irrelevant, standard of behavior that most people feel they can't live up to.

Consequently, Odets is engaged in a war on current AIDS-prevention programmes – Use a Condom Every Time – which he compares to slick advertising campaigns. 'We are not addressing the human needs of the gay community by offering or insisting upon biological survival as the exclusive purpose of human life,' he writes. Such a statement must be startling to people who are not, like Odets, deeply involved with a self-identified gay male urban American community, some of whose members are his patients. Odets is suggesting that in such a community, like the one in San Francisco, where half the people are HIV-infected, there is a different relationship to death, and to life expectancy.

In other words, being gay in San Francisco (and in New York, and Los Angeles, and Houston and Miami and Chicago) in the 1990s is profoundly depressing, if you find it depressing to realize that half your friends, and maybe you yourself, will be dead by the time your reach forty. Odets is suggesting that it's reasonable, under the circumstances, for people to take relatively small sexual risks. That's hard for me to accept. During the two weeks I'm in San Francisco, I never really shake the conviction that anybody who has unprotected sex in America in 1995, especially anal or vaginal sex, without proof that both partners are HIV-negative, is an idiot. A selfish idiot, because when you die, you don't die alone, you pull all your friends and family and loved ones into the almost unwatchably painful, messy drama of your slow death from AIDS.

But in San Francisco, the unwatchably painful is commonplace, even inevitable. According to Castro-area psychotherapist Tom Moon, some HIV-negative people are so certain they'll eventually die of AIDS that when they finally test HIV-positive they are actually relieved. 'At least they don't have to worry anymore about when it's going to happen', he explains.

It seems to me that the pre-infection anxiety about when you're going to be exposed can't be as bad as the post-infection anxiety about when you are going to get sick and die, but when I point this out to Moon, he looks at me as if I'm missing the point. We're sitting in his sunny office near Noe Street, a few blocks away from the hectic, touristy, homo-utopian business district of Castro Street. Moon, a forty-seven-year-old man with a clipped white beard and

20

wire-frame glasses obscuring a round, placid face, is explaining why it's crucial to rewrite AIDS-prevention programs. 'They tell you to use a condom every time', he says, 'to *always* play safe. Well, the only thing that leaves out is human psychology'.

One of the crucial and necessary goals of 1980 AIDS activist movements was to protect and promote the rights of HIV-positive people, and to show how normal their lives were, despite the disease. Maybe, Moon suggests, the campaign worked too well. Testing HIV-positive in 1995, is nowhere near as terrifying as getting an AIDS diagnosis in 1985, when it was still considered a death sentence. If you were lucky, you had two years to live. That was before long-term survivors, before AZT. It was before movies like *Philadelphia* and *Boys on the Side* made AIDS look heroic and sweet. Moon feels that HIV infection has been dangerously glamorized, making role models out of people who were dying.

'I remember back at the beginning of the disease', Moon says, 'one of my closest friends was among the first one hundred people to die, and he was canonized as a saint. Well, he wasn't heroic at all, he was just sick'. People are so freaked out about death and dying that they cast sick friends as martyrs and saints, even when they act, in sickness, like curmudgeons. This is especially true in the gay community, where so many have died during the past fifteen years that you'd expect people to be less mystical, and more practical, about death. Just because hundreds of gay men have died heroically doesn't mean every death is heroic.

Moon feels that heroism may lie more in remaining HIV-negative than in going through the long, protracted, heartbreaking process of dying from AIDS. 'All the messages out there', he says, 'all the outreach programs and the billboards and the safe-sex pamphlets are aimed at people who are HIV-positive, and it sends a clear message to people who are not'. The message, Moon says, is that in order to be truly gay in San Francisco, it is necessary to be HIV-positive .

21

I feel skeptical about this claim, though I remember something Eric Rofes said to me: 'Maybe the more people merge with the gay community, the more strongly they identify themselves as gay men, the more likely they are to get HIV-infected; while the more likely the further away they are from merging with the community, the longer they stay negative'. Rofes also told me about support groups that are forming in San Francisco for HIV-negative people. You can go to an HIV-negative potluck brunch, or attend HIV-negative group therapy sessions. 'I don't know exactly what my *issues* as an HIV-negative man might be', a friend of mine says when I mention HIV-negative support groups, 'since I'm not the one who might be dying'. Another friend admits he was invited to a brunch but didn't go because, though he believes Moon is right about the needs of HIV-negative people, he 'felt creepy about going to a brunch'.

No one wants to set up a nasty competition between HIV-negative and HIV-positive people. Nevertheless, there is the clear and disturbing sense that sickness has been normalized. 'Disability insurance is an NEA fellowship for queers', jokes Justin Chin, a twenty-five-year-old performance artist. Then there is this story of Kerrington Osborne's: 'When I first moved to San Francisco, I went to a party with a couple of friends, and we sat around the room and introduced ourselves. We talked about AIDS . And my friends and I, who were all like twenty-six or twenty-seven at the time, didn't know anyone with HIV or AIDS. Well, the people at the party looked at us and said, "Give it two more years and you will". And two years later, we did'.

Elliot Ramos says to me: 'Haven't you ever had sex with someone you love, and you're in the middle of things, and you don't want to stop and mess with a condom or think about AIDS – you want it to be, like, seamless and perfect, like it is in the movies?'. Well, yes and no. In fact I haven't dated in a year and a half, and I haven't had sex without a phone receiver in six months. I've never had anal sex without a condom, except once with my last boyfriend, after we'd been together six months and he tested negative for about the fifteenth time. That was three years ago. I haven't had oral sex with ejaculation since the first guy I was ever in love with in 1983, when I was twenty-four and he was otherwise so sexually conservative it was like dating the Immaculate Conception.

Then in the middle of writing this story, I met, you know, this guy. And frankly, I want to have sex with him without worrying so much about disease. So I'm getting tested again. I'm sitting in an empty doctor's office in New York with my sleeve rolled up, holding a cotton swab to the inside of my elbow and waiting for the blood to return to my head. Being punctured makes me queasy. I don't mind the pinprick of the needle. What bothers me is my blood. The thought of it makes me light-headed and nauseated. I've been tested five times, and every time I have to sit down with my head between my knees for ten minutes afterward, not because of AIDS anxiety, but because I don't like having veins. When I was in college I said grandly that I was glad I wasn't straight, because I'd never need a blood test to get married. As it turns out, being gay means I have to get tested just to go on a date.

Dating 1990s AIDS style: my possible new boyfriend is in the reception room, holding my knapsack. I've known him a month and a half. We've been talking about being tested together for the past two weeks, but I was like, 'Let's not move too fast. I mean, I haven't even seen his high-school yearbook yet'. The HIV test is a mating ritual, it's a commitment, like Ann-Margret wearing her boyfriend's fraternity pin in *Bye Bye Birdie*. I wasn't ready to be pinned. Except here I am. A grown man with a hole in his arm and the unreasonable faith that, if we both test negative, the losses of the past ten years will be redeemed, and my youth will be returned to me somehow. Testing negative for the first time is like becoming a virgin again. By the sixth time, however, it's a reminder that your luck can change in an instant, and that nothing, not new love and certainly not your life, is guaranteed.

I'll offend my friends with HIV and AIDS if I say that I've made up my mind – I'm testing HIV-positive. Maybe I have nothing to worry about, but still, I don't like tempting fate. Expect the worst, I think, and you'll never be disappointed. What if I test HIV-positive? Will I turn into a political zealot? AIDS activism is full of born-again radicals, people who've been transformed by sero-conversion. They admit that they didn't care who was HIV-infected until they got infected themselves. But I don't need to test HIV-positive in order to know what it's like to cope with that anxiety.

There is, after all, still such a thing as empathy, though identity politics has nearly killed it off. According to identity politics, no one is supposed to be able to understand what anyone else is going through. Each of us is a sealed heart, locked inside a box of minority status. Perhaps the last round of AIDS activism fizzled because it was based on a similarly cynical notion: that self-interest dictates behavior. I'm not going to care about your agony until it becomes my own. Of course, that leaves out compassion, and the possibility of human touch, and knowing what it means to suffer without putting yourself through every single kind of pain.

'You can't know how this feels', a friend who recently tested HIV-positive told me, and while I don't want to sound disrespectful, I think he's wrong. I know dread and loss, and I know fear about the future, and I know about living daily with the sense that what I can't stand to give up is going to be taken from me too soon. What I want to say to my friend is that he doesn't have to reinvent himself as the member of some minority group to attract my sympathy and win my support. And I don't have to sit in an overlit doctor's office pretending I'm HIV-positive in order to know what being infected meant. As it turns out, the doctor comes back in the room and tells me I tested negative. But if I tested HIV-positive, I would at least have some idea of what to expect.

To answer Elliot's questions: Yes, I want to be forgetful, and sometimes, deliberately, I am. On the other hand, there is this: of all the ways to die in America at the end of the twentieth century – industrial poisoning, cancer from radiation, nuclear meltdown, drive-by death, drug overdose, spousal abuse – AIDS is the last one I would choose. It's an appalling death. Everybody seems to be forgetting that. It isn't like a Tom Hanks movie – you don't get hugged by Antonio Banderas and gently expire while Joanne Woodward weeps for you in the corner. It takes forever, and you won't win an Oscar for putting yourself through it. Instead, you'll turn into a skeleton slowly, achingly, over time, and lose your job, your money, your lovers, your eyesight, your appetite, your bowel control, your memory, your mind. You'll rage and scream, you'll alienate all your friends and family and ruin their love for you and destroy your regard for yourself. I would rather step on a land mine in Vietnam and die with my body parts hanging in a tree. I can live with a condom.

Chapter Three

GOING IN
John Weir

This will kill my parents and ruin my career, but listen, I take it back: I'm not gay. I don't mean I don't still fall in love with guys, or that I wouldn't be willing to go to a gay rights demonstration if I thought it would enhance someone's civil liberties. I never said I was straight. However, for most of my adult life I've insisted on being thought of as a gay man, and I just want to say right now that I'm over it. Big deal, I'm homosexual. According to identity politics, however, my sexuality is all important. It sets me apart from the mainstream. Well, duh, I never felt like part of the mainstream anyway. Not when it seemed to be filled exclusively with scary straight men, and not now, either, when it's making room for scary gay ones.

It used to be an insult to accuse a guy of acting gay. Lately, it's discreet praise. It means he's sensitive, really well-dressed and probably friends with someone who knows Barbra Streisand. Accepting an Oscar for his role as a dying fag in *Philadelphia*, Tom Hanks even managed to make homosexuality sound patriotic. 'God bless America', he said, weeping for dead gay men like they were Veterans of Foreign Wars. Recently, the most unlikely people have been cashing in on queer visibility, from Robert Altman, who is planning a screen version of playwright Tony Kushner's homo-anthem *Angels in America*, to Stephen Spielberg, who produced the drag extravaganza *To Wong Foo, Thanks for Everything, Julie Newmar* as if it were an all-American family entertainment.

Homosexuality is being repackaged and resold to Americans as a traditional family value. And homosexuals are emerging as the yuppies of the 1990s. They're the new class of urban professionals with money to spend and aggressively marketed products to choose from. Absolut Vodka, Ikea, Benetton, Dewar's, Calvin Klein, Levis 501s, Brad Pitt and Nine Inch Nails are just a few of the commodities secretly or openly aimed at upwardly mobile, straight-acting, white-appearing gay guys and the handful of lesbians with comparable economic power. It's not enough to say that these people are patsies to a culture that takes their money without granting them their rights. The sad fact is that homosexuals are desperate to be exploited.

If you read any of the new or newly mainstream advertising-laden gay magazines, *Out* or *The Advocate* or *Genre*, or if you saw the thousands of identically clad homosexuals who flooded New York City during the June 1994 Stonewall 25 celebration, you know where the gay community is headed. It's not moving towards legal rights. It's not focused on mourning its dead, or insisting self-preservingly on safer sex, or on finding a cure for breast cancer or AIDS. The collective impulse of the chic lesbians and the brave young gay Republicans who captivate the media today and titillate each other is shopping.

That's what the gay magazines are for, to target and create a consumer demographic. Their interest isn't politics of sexuality. Indeed, they're so worried about offending their few loyal corporate advertisers with copy that is too sexy or political that the only thing homosexual about them is their shame. They tell the world that the characteristic homosexual act is compulsive spending. Otherwise, they're merely a cheerleading squad for anything gay or remotely gay-friendly, no matter how banal. If Melissa Etheridge burps, she gets covered in the gay press. Then there are the 'gay leaders' who show up on the covers of gay magazines: Roseanne. Bill Clinton. Barbra Streisand. Marky Mark. During New York's 1995 Gay Pride week, *The Advocate* put New York Republican Mayor Rudolph

Giuliani on its cover, which is like putting Joseph Mengele on the front page of *Hadassah* magazine on Yom Kippur.

Streisand of course is ubiquitous. Does everyone who has ever had a homosexual impulse owe her a personal thank-you? For what? For directing George Carlin to play a sissygirl faggot in *The Prince of Tides*? For leaving out of the film the lesbianism that was central to the book? Homosexuals are suffering from a collective case of Stockholm syndrome – falling in love with our tormentors. How else to explain what makes Marky Mark a gay icon, except that he looks like the guy from high school gym class who spent half his time exciting your ashamed desire, and the other half shutting your head in his locker? Self-identified gay men lament that they have no national leaders, that the community can't 'support' its leadership, that the gay rights movement is too diverse and mistrusting, too 'hurt' to walk behind a representative figure. But I don't know a fag who wouldn't follow Marky Mark into a firing squad if he so much as winked.

Gay magazines still arrive in your mailbox in discreet wrapping, if you request it. But it would be far more startling for your neighbours and mail carriers to learn that you subscribe to truly politically radical and sex-obsessed journals, like bulletins from the religious right. Actually, there are a lot of similarities between the gay rights movement and Christian fundamentalism. Like homosexuals, Christians are increasingly open about their practices. Like some fervent queer activists, many Christians are shrill, dogmatic, paranoiac, combative and separatist. The difference is that while Christians rally around God, homosexuals only have sex. You don't have to look your best to win God's love, but if you're searching for a gay man, you'd better have tits. Gay men are such a straining, susceptible horde of self-loathing, hump-happy pleasure seekers that anyone with a decent set of biceps and a smidgen of media savvy could lead them where no fascist, or televangelist, has ever gone before.

The entire gay male community seems at times to be colluding against the possibility of independent thinking. The gay rights movement, too often, is focused on theatrics rather than on discourse: we want to be entertained and flattered, not criticized. As a group, self-identified gay men are especially resistant to thinking about issues of class and race, and they steadfastly deny their sexism. The irony of gay liberation is that it has made room in the mainstream only for those white men who are already privileged, and disinclined to share their wealth. This is the charge that many Christian fundamentalists make against us: that we are a bunch of affluent men who think our homosexuality shouldn't interfere with our God-given right to rule the world. Fundamentalists aren't exactly strangers to feeling both martyred and entitled, of course. Maybe that's why, in vilifying us, they're partly right.

There was a time in my early twenties when being gay meant everything to me. I felt like my sexuality explained my entire life. It was the missing puzzle piece which, clicked into place, finally brought the whole picture into focus. The ten years after I came out, at age twenty-three, were a very heady time. I marched in Gay Pride celebrations throughout the 1980s. I got arrested for protesting because homosexuals weren't allowed to join New York City's St Patrick's Day parade. I went to ACT UP meetings and networked with all the smartest, cutest, most energetic dykes and fags in Manhattan, and thus, I thought naively, in the world. I hooked up with Queer Nation and raided straight bars. I remember one night precisely: we went to a skinhead dive in the East Village and kissed each other every fifteen minutes. There were no skinheads in the bar that night – the bar, in fact, was nearly empty – but it was a thrilling thing to do. It felt redemptive. It felt like I was facing down everyone who had ever called me 'faggot' in high school and saying 'Yeah so?'.

That part of my life was important to my self-respect. I won't disavow the years when I wore 'QUEER NATION' T-shirts or pinned pink triangles to my lapel. Lately, however, I want to trade all my gay paraphernalia for a button that says 'NOT ME'. I'm postgay, a counterqueer, the ungrateful beneficiary of the gains of gay liberation. It's not just that I'm frustrated with the mindlessness of the gay male community, and the elitism of its leadership. I've decided to reject the whole category of 'gay'. Lately, I've been agreeing with Gore Vidal. In his introduction to the 1963 edition of his infamous 1948 homo novel *The City and the Pillar*, he says 'There is of course no such thing as a homosexual. Despite current usage, the word is an adjective describing a sexual action, not a noun describing a recognizable type'.

Theoretically, Vidal is right. Effectively, however, there is currently no more recognizable type than the self-identified, politically active, sexually predatory gay American man, the kind of guy who wants, not equality for everyone, but entitlement for himself. And big pecs. If gay men ruled America, there would be tax credits for joining a gym. This was abundantly clear to me at the New York Stonewall 25 celebration, the twenty-fifth anniversary of the uprising that inspired the gay rights movement. It was a week-long festival of pod people twirling their multi-colored freedom rings. There were so many hairless young men in nipple-hugging white T-shirts wandering the streets, that I began to wish that it was 1969 again and paddy wagons would come and take them all away.

I spent the week with my best friend, the writer David B. Feinberg, who was dying of AIDS. He was having a hard time eating. Parasites were wearing away the undulant walls of his intestines, and he couldn't keep anything down. Wherever we went, our main concern was finding the john. As it happened, when I wasn't with David, I was reporting a magazine article about aspiring gay male porn stars. I went from club to club with members of my community, bare-chested men in cut-off blue jeans and black combat boots. Gay liberation has made it possible for every male homosexual in America to look the same and act too beautiful to talk to. If David had come along, he would have looked around the dance floor and said, 'Cute boy, cute boy, cute boy'. But David was home shitting his beauty into the toilet, and the cute boys he might have wanted were busy trying to look like storm troopers.

In our fervour to be part of the mainstream, we are creating stereotypes about ourselves that are just as clichéd as anything the religious right might dream up. This is evident in openly gay playwright Terence McNally's *Love! Valour! Compassion!*, a recent Tony Award winning Broadway hit. The play concerns some upwardly mobile, well-dressed gay white men – artists and per- formers and urban professionals – who spend summer weekends together at a lovely country house in upstate New York. They swim, play tennis, make meals, serenade each other on the piano with Chopin waltzes, sunbathe nude, lament about AIDS and finally, triumphantly, dress up in tutus and dance to *Swan Lake*.

The play is full of sentimental notions of gay male solidarity: all gay men, except for the ones who know about musical comedy, have beautiful bodies; they are all epicures; they love to sit outside in the sun; if they're bitchy it's only because they're wounded; if they die it's somebody else's fault. Their pain is cured by women's clothing. Their desire is aroused, most fervently, by Puerto Ricans. Of course, there is an equally sentimental and misleading version of the 1990s male homosexual as an angry young queer. Picture a line of brave protesters confronting police officers in riot gear. The activists' faces are contorted in rage. 'We're here, we're queer, get used to it', they chant, their voices raised as one in agonized lament.

I have been such a radical queer, and I have spent cozy weekends at some rich man's country house, eating gourmet food and talking politics and art. It's easy for me to spend time in both camps, because they are essentially the same. Nevertheless, critics from both sides support a false distinction between them. In *A Place at the*

31

Table, self-identified 'conservative' gay writer Bruce Bawer contrasts 'subculture' gays with conservative ones, 'elegantly turned out' gay men who go to church on Sunday. Radical queers say Bawer is self-loathing and anti-sex. But the two groups are haggling over style, not ideology. Both Bawer and Queer Nation belong to the privileged upper tenth of the gay community, the class of urban artists and professionals who dictate gay politics to the rest of the country. There are no statistics to prove it, of course, but if mainstream means 'majority', I bet the mainstream of homosexuality in America today is in the Marines.

And in the Navy. And living on public assistance in Idaho. And leaving Latin American enclaves in Los Angeles to cruise for wealthy gringos wearing beautiful sweaters in gay bars lining Santa Monica Boulevard. The mainstream of homosexuality in America today is living at home with Mom and Dad in a two-family house in Whitestone, Queens, acting 'straight' all day with friends held over from high school, but getting on homosexual phone-sex lines at night and saying things like, 'Anybody out there like a lot of body contact?'. Mainstream homosexuals are straight guys who go to gay bars once a week on Fridays and warn their girlfriends not to ask them what they're doing on their one night out. They are lesbians whose order of preference for sexual partners is: (1) straight women, (2) bisexual men, (3) other lesbians.

Yet the gay community represented in Ikea ads, the comfy image of a couple of middle-class white guys out shopping for furniture, is the one that has been identified as the mainstream. It's a lie. It is a lie for which radical dykes and fags are just as culpable as assimilationist lesbians and gays. The true division in the gay community is between the entrenched, privileged, politically active urban and suburban trend-setters and policy makers, and the mass of people with homosexual urges who feel represented more by *Reader's Digest* and *Soldier of Fortune* magazine than by *The*

Advocate or *Genre* or *10 Percent* or *Frontiers* or *Deneuve* or *On Our Backs* or *Out*. If indeed they have even heard of them.

Nothing reveals the self-absorption of the gay ruling class more patently and damningly than its response to the problems of being homosexual in the military. Radical gays, hiding behind a veneer of pacifism, are especially guilty of classism and elitism in this instance. During the 1993 debate about President Clinton's proposal to lift the ban on gays in the military, radical queers very nearly colluded with anti-gay politicos, like Georgia Senator Sam Nunn, who organized the Congessional hearings on tolerating homosexuals in the armed forces. 'If they're in the military, they get what they deserve', homo radicals told me, over and over, throughout the hearings.

Knee-jerk anti-military feeling dictated the radicals' official response. And a widespread and often petty mistrust of journalist Randy Shilts prevented the radical homo community from taking into account Shilts' devastating 1993 study of gay life in the military, *Conduct Unbecoming*. Shilts recounts severe and repeated civil rights violations, inflicted by military brass on gays or suspected gays, most of them women and/or African-American. The practice of homo witch-hunting actually intensified during the 1980s, roughly paralleling the AIDS crisis and ruining thousands of lives. But the activist gay community largely ignored the evidence in Shilts' book, because many gay men were still sulking over Shilts' role in closing gay bathhouses in San Francisco in the early 1980s.

It's more important to get blown by a grunt in public than it is to defend his civil rights. Fags like to fetishize marines, in part because of their mostly working-class appeal. But if somebody in the armed forces complains about how the military treats him, a lot of gay men tune out. 'Abolish the military altogether', radical fags say, overlooking the fact that enlisting in the armed forces is often the most viable economic alternative for working-class young men. If you're seventeen-years-old and you don't like musical comedy, and you don't want to move to New York or Chicago or Los Angeles, and you don't have enough money for college; and if you know that you like sweaty, male environments; and if you want to get the hell out of your small town, why not the Marines? Not every gay man in America is a chorus boy or a sensitive poet or a Harvard MBA.

Of course, there were plenty of gay lawyers and Washington lobbyists who did try to help gays in the military. But they were defeated by a false sense of security. They assumed that because they were middle-class white guys they would naturally get what they wanted. The gay rights movement, from radicals to conservatives, is crippled by a sense of entitlement. Sometimes I think the difference between the two factions is just a question of contrasting fashion statements. In either case, I'm no longer dressing for either party. I'm sick of gay men. The next time I see a bunch of dudes from Jersey beating on a faggot from Greenwich Village, I'm going to cheer them on. Being gay used to feel like an expression of difference, but I lost my otherness, and now I want it back. I'm not gay any more. I'm not even queer. I'd almost rather be mistaken for a registered Republican. After all, there's no distinction anymore between conservative Republicans and self-identified homosexuals. A conservative is someone who wants to keep what he has. So is a gay man. The gay rights movement is largely helmed by white men who crave what they were promised as children, but denied as adults because of their sexuality; they want their guaranteed access to power. And they're not necessarily interested in extending that power to you, just because you happen to like having sex, sometimes, with guys.

Chapter Four

IT'S JUST A PHASE:
WHY HOMOSEXUALITY IS DOOMED
Peter Tatchell

• The ultimate queer emancipation is the abolition of homosexuality and the eradication of the homosexual.

One of the most enduring put-downs of homosexual desire, beloved of so many parents and psychiatrists, is that our queerness is a temporary aberration. It's just a phase we're going through, they tell us. We'll soon grow out of it and eventually embrace a happy, healthy heterosexuality. At least that's what they hope.

Some people do find that homosexuality is restricted to a limited period of their lives, such as in teenage experimentation or a brief mid-life affair. For these men and women, queer sex is a genuinely transient encounter.

But that is not the experience of most lesbians and gays whose same-sex attraction feels eternal and lasts a lifetime. There is nothing momentary about the sense that being gay is something that has always been part of us and will remain integral to our sexual and emotional feelings.

It would, however, be a mistake to confuse personal experience of queer desire with the cultural evolution of queerness over time. The two are not the same. The difference lies in the tension between homosexuality as we individually and subjectively live it, and homosexuality as an objective social phenomenon that develops and changes during the passage of history. For those of us who feel certain and confident in our homosexuality, the idea that these feelings are a phase is profoundly insulting. Yet, historically-speaking, homosexuality is indeed just that. Like every other expression of human culture, homosexuality as we know it hasn't always existed and won't last forever. Our modern Western forms of lesbian and gay identity, sexual behaviour, relationship patterns and sub-culture are relatively recent developments. The notion of queers as a group of people distinct from straights is notably new.

Just as surely as the contemporary configuration of homo-sexuality and homosexuals arose from a certain moment in social development, one day it will also fade away. So will heterosexuality and heterosexuals, as we currently understand them. In a future, more enlightened and emancipated epoch, the present separate, exclusive and rigid sexualities of straight and gay will be supplanted by a more all-inclusive, polymorphous and fluid sexuality. People will no longer define themselves as hetero or homo, and the gender of a person's sexual partner will cease to determine the social validity, or illegitimacy, of their carnal and affectional feelings.

What makes this sexual transformation a possibility is the fact that sexuality is like any other cultural artefact. Influenced by social values and personal judgements, it can and does change from era to era. Different socio-economic circumstances and moral climates affect the way eroticism is expressed. Sexual relationships that are common or acceptable in one century may not be so in others. Manifestations of sexuality can also vary enormously between different cultures. The homosexuality of present-day Western societies is, for example, quite unlike the homosexuality of Ancient Greece and Imperial China.

That contemporary patterns of queer desire are culturally-specific and historically evolving can be seen in the emergence of gay relationships between adults of equal social status over the last three hundred years. Previously, most same-sex attachments had been between an older and younger person, often involving elements of a teacher/pupil relationship. Or they tended to be between a powerful ruler or benefactor and someone of inferior, dependent social standing. The historical emergence of homosexual relationships on a more egalitarian plane begs the question: if homosexuality has not been always like it is today, surely it can just as easily change again in the future?

Another relatively recent development is the way people who are erotically attracted to others of the same sex now define themselves in terms of their sexuality. This embracing of a gay identity had its beginnings in eighteenth-century European cities. Prior to that time, individuals did not describe themselves according to their sexual orientation. There were only homosexual acts, not homosexual people (even the word 'homosexual' was not coined until the mid-nineteenth century). Thus the notion of 'the homosexual' as a distinct category of person has not been around forever.

Just as there was a time in the past when homosexuals did not exist (only people who had sex with others of the same gender), perhaps there will also come a moment in the future when the word 'homosexual' will stop being the definition of a type of person and describe merely a form of behaviour. In other words, 'the homosexual' will cease to exist.

Ironically, the medieval Catholic Church, for all its obscurantism and intolerance, was close to the mark. Homosexuality was not, it suggested, the special sin of a unique class of people but a dangerous temptation to which any mortal might succumb. This doctrine implicitly conceded the attractiveness of same-sex desire, and unwittingly acknowledged its pervasive, universal potential.

Subsequent research indicates that most people are indeed born with a sexual desire that is, to varying degrees, capable of both heterosexual and homosexual attraction. The sociological surveys of Dr Alfred Kinsey in the United States during the 1940s and 1950s uncovered evidence that heterosexuality and homosexuality are not watertight, contradictory and irreconcilable sexual orientations. He found that sexuality is a continuum of desires and behaviours, ranging from exclusive heterosexuality to exclusive homosexuality. A substantial proportion of the population is somewhere in the middle, sharing an amalgam of same-sex and opposite-sex feelings. In *Sexual Behaviour in the Human Male* (1948), Kinsey recorded that 13 per cent of the men he surveyed were either mostly or exclusively homosexual for at least three years between the ages of sixteen and fifty-five. Twenty-five per cent had more than incidental gay reactions or experience, amounting to clear and continuing same-sex desires. Altogether, 37 per cent of the men Kinsey questioned had experienced sex with other males to the point of orgasm at least once, and half had experienced mental attraction or erotic arousal towards other men (sometimes transient and not physically expressed). Kinsey's companion research, *Sexual Behaviour in the Human Female* (1953), found the incidence of homosexuality and bisexuality among women was about half that of men. This discrepancy can perhaps be explained by the prevailing misogynistic culture, which tended to encourage women's dependence on men and thereby restrict opportunities for the development of an autonomous female sexuality.

The Kinsey research has since been criticized as unrepresentative, largely on the basis that instead of being randomized and weighted to reflect a true cross-section of the US population, it relied too heavily on self-selected volunteer interviewees and on sampling from often single-sex institutions like colleges, prisons and the armed forces. Kinsey's statistics have also been called into question by the results of recent sexological investigations, such as The National Survey of Sexual Attitudes and Lifestyles. Carried out in the UK from 1990 to 1991 and published under the title *Sexual Behaviour in Britain* (1992), it found significantly lower levels of same-sex relations. Only 6.1 per cent of men and 3.4 per cent of women reported having had a homosexual experience during their lifetime.

The methodology of this survey has, however, been severely criticized. It was based on a random geographic sample of the population. Yet we know that homosexuals are not randomly distributed across the country. They tend to be concentrated in big cities, and in particular districts within those cities. Moreover, the interviews took place in people's homes. Closeted lesbians, gays and bisexuals are unlikely to admit same-sex behaviour to a stranger who knocks on their door, especially if they live with their families and fear exposure. For these reasons, the researchers felt obliged to add the following caveat to their findings: 'Since homosexual sex is stigmatized in Britain, it can expect to be under- rather than over-reported . . . all prevalence figures relating to homosexual activity should be regarded as minimum estimates'.

A number of other recent sex research projects have produced statistics at variance with those of *The National Survey:*

● Polling by the British Marketing Research Bureau for the Health Education Authority in 1989 discovered that 86.5 per cent of men and women had 'never' felt attracted to a person of the same sex. Thirteen and a half per cent had either experienced homosexual attraction (7.5 per cent) or declined to answer the question (6 per cent). This exceptionally high refusal rate suggests that some of those who declined may have been lesbians, gays or bisexuals, afraid to admit their same-sex desires.

● In 1989, the United States Committee on AIDS Research reported that 20 per cent of American men had had homosexual sex and that 3.3 per cent had these experiences 'fairly often' or 'occasionally'.

● A French compilation of questionnaire results on a range of subjects published in the same year, *Vous les Français: 56 Millions de Français en 2200 Sondages*, revealed that 25 per cent of French men claimed to have had sex with another man.

● The American *National Health and Social Life Survey*, which was published in 1994, found that only 2.4 per cent of men and 1.3 per cent of women define themselves as homosexual or bisexual. Nonetheless, 10 per cent of the males and 9 per cent of the females said they had either desired or experienced sexual relations with a person of the same sex.

These figures suggest that while Kinsey may have over-estimated the incidence of same-sex relations, the recent British research in *The National Survey* has almost certainly under-reported it.

What is crucial to the argument concerning the future social evolution of sexuality is not the current prevalence of homosexual and bisexual behaviour, but the instrinsic human capability and potentiality for greater sexual diversity. Although the frequency of same-sex relations adduced by Kinsey has been contradicted by some contemporary surveys, what these new surveys do not challenge is the notion of a spectrum of sexuality, within which significant numbers of people experience both hetero and homo affinity.

The National Survey found that 4.8 per cent of men and 2.5 per cent of women had had both gay and straight experiences. Even these small percentages translate into over 1.5 million British people with bisexual histories.

The authors of *The National Survey* freely acknowledge the value of Kinsey's ground-breaking theorization of sexuality as a spectrum of diverse and often overlapping desires: 'The polarity "homosexual – heterosexual" is an inadequate categorization of the population; same and opposite-gender sexual expression are better represented as a continuum'. They concluded: 'Very substantial proportions of those reporting same-sex partners also report opposite sex partners ... Of men who report having ever had a male sexual partner in their lifetime, 90.3% have also had a female sexual partner, and for women the equivalent proportion is 95.8%'.

The possibility that individuals could share a capacity for both hetero and homo feelings was an idea that Sigmund Freud promoted. His psychoanalytic investigations led him to argue, in *Three Essays on the Theory of Sexuality* (1905) and *An Autobiographical Study* (1925), that everyone is born with a 'constitutional bisexuality', possessing both a heterosexual and a homosexual capability.

Erotic desires are initially pluralistic and diverse, without any differentiation between attraction to male and female. Sexual orientation evolves, Freud theorized, through a complex developmental process which is significantly influenced by social factors, such as relationship with parents during infancy and the moral norms dictated by society. Socialization, rather than biologically innate preference, is the pivotal force in the formation of sexuality, according to Freud. Writing in *Psycho-Analytic Notes on an Autobiographical Account of a Case of Paranoia* (1911), he argued that 'every human being oscillates all through his life between heterosexual and homosexual feelings'. Freud's case histories of *Little Hans* (1909) and *Dora* (1905) led him to note that he had never conducted a single case of psychoanalysis 'without having to take into account a very considerable current of homosexuality'. He observed that 'latent or unconscious homosexuality can be detected in all normal people'.

If queerness is intrinsic to human sexuality, then it has the potential to be much more commonplace than it is currently. What prevents this is social homophobia. Although he did so rather cautiously and circuitously, Freud acknowledged the cultural suppression of homosexuality. His *Fragment of an Analysis of a Case of Hysteria* (1905) contrasts the denigration of homosexuals in Western societies with their frequent acceptance by 'different races and different epochs'. In *Three Essays on the Theory of Sexuality*, he added that sexual repression was substantially the result of the 'structures of morality and authority erected by society'. The intimation is that the existing sexual order is mostly man-made and could therefore be modified by human will and effort.

Cultural conditioning as an explanation for homosexuality is supported by the findings of the anthropologists Clellan Ford and Frank Beach. In *Patterns of Sexual Behaviour* (1965) they noted that certain forms of homosexuality were considered normal and acceptable in forty-nine (nearly two-thirds) of the seventy-six tribal societies surveyed from the 1920s to the 1950s. They also recorded details of some aboriginal cultures, such as the Keraki and Sambia of Papua New Guinea, where all young men entered into a homosexual relationship with an unmarried male warrior, sometimes lasting several years, as part of their rites of passage into manhood. Once completed, they ceased all homosexual contact and assumed sexual relations with women. If sexual orientation was biologically preprogrammed, these men would have never been able to switch to homosexuality and then to heterosexuality with such apparent ease. This led Ford and Beach to deduce that homosexuality is 'the product of the fundamental mammalian heritage of general sexual responsiveness as modified under the impact of experience'. In other words, the potential for erotic attraction to both sexes is fundamental to the human species.

The evidence from these three research disciplines – sociology, psychology and anthropology – is that sexual orientations are not fixed and mutually exclusive. There is a good deal of movement and overlap. What's more, although sexuality may be partly affected by biological predispositions – such as genes, hormones and possibly brain structures – the decisive causal factors appear to be childhood experiences, social expectations, peer pressure and moral values. These are the key determinants that channel our erotic impulses in certain directions and not others. This means that our sexual orientation is culturally constructed, not biologically given. Rather than being solidified and immutable, it is, in our formative first few

years of life, to a very significant extent, open-ended and malleable.
If sexual attraction is not predestined, then it has the potentiality to develop in either a queer or a straight direction, or in both directions simultaneously. We already know from various sexual surveys that even in our intensely homophobic culture a sizeable proportion of the population experiences both hetero and homo arousal. That evidence comes from surveys that record *consciously* recognized desires. At the level of unconscious feeling – where passions are often displaced, sublimated, projected and transferred – it seems probable that very few people are 100 per cent straight or gay. Most are a mixture. Human sexuality is much more complex, diverse and blurred than the traditional simplistic binary image of hetero and homo, so beloved of straight moralists and – significantly – most lesbians and gay men.

Since sexual orientation has a culturally influenced element of indeterminacy, fluidity and plasticity, the present forms of homosexuality and heterosexuality are unlikely to remain the same in perpetuity. What has changed in the past can also change in the future. This offers the prospect of a homosexuality that is quite different from the homosexuality we know today. Perhaps, eventually, there will come a moment in the development of human civilization when defining oneself as lesbian or gay will cease to have relevance or meaning. Maybe homosexuality as a distinct and exclusive sexual orientation will be transcended – as will its mirror opposite, heterosexuality. Instead, the vast majority of people will be open to the possibility of both opposite-sex and same-sex fancies and no one will give a damn about who loves and lusts after whom.

It is not such an implausible dream. Sooner or later, discrimination in law against lesbians and gay men will be abolished and legal equality for homosexuals finally won (probably within fifty years in Britain and the US). When prejudiced attitudes are eradicated and there is genuine social acceptance of queers (which may take considerably longer), the differences between heterosexuals and homosexuals will cease to have any social significance. With heterosexuality stripped of its connotations of superiority – the idea that straight is better and more deserving than gay – the distinction between the two orientations will become progressively more hazy and irrelevant. Once homophobic prejudice and repression are abandoned, the need to distinguish between gay and straight disappears.

The only reason there currently exists a hetero/homo divide, with competing identities and behaviours, is because one form of sexuality has been deemed more valid than the other. The division exists to reinforce and perpetuate that value judgement. Society has determined that 'the homosexual' must be labelled and pilloried as someone separate from 'the heterosexual' in order to contain and control same-sex desire, which it variously deems to be unnatural, perverted, immoral, sick, abnormal and inferior. Homosexuality is thus a categorization invented by straights to marginalize and constrain queer love within an identifiable, demonized minority. The gay/straight schism, by marking queers out as distinct (and devalued) human beings, helps sustain our oppression. This means it is not in the interests of lesbians and gay men to maintain barriers based on sexual difference. Our liberation is irrevocably bound up with the dissolution of separate, mutually exclusive, rival orientations and identities.

The prerequisite for overcoming the hetero/homo conflict is tackling the reason for its existence: the denial of the right to sexual difference. We therefore have to assert the right of queers to be different and to celebrate the virtues of sexual differentiation. In a homophobic society, normalizing homosexuality is the precondition for the abolition of the straight/gay antagonism. When we are being attacked because we are gay, we have to defend our gayness. To reach a state of affairs where no one cares who's queer and who's straight, we first have to challenge and defeat those homophobes who care very much and who make erotic otherness the basis for the denial of respect and human rights. This is the supreme paradox. Only when sexual difference is fully accepted and valued will it cease to be important and consequently slide into oblivion. Homosexuality, and all the differences it embodies compared to heterosexuality, must thus be defended and promoted in order for it to be ultimately transcended. Whether we like it or not, our every success in emancipating queers from oppression hastens the demise of homosexuality as a separate, exclusive identity and behaviour. Winning moral legitimacy and legal equality for lesbians and gay men undermines the whole hetero/homo polarity, diluting the differences between the two sexualities and weakening the cultural significance attributed to those differences.

Without first securing the social validation of same-sex love it is impossible to create a society where the differences between straight and gay no longer matter. As long as homophobic prejudice and discrimination exist, the differences will, quite understandably, continue to matter a great deal to the homosexuals and bisexuals who suffer as a consequence. Those differences can only begin to dim and die once there is genuine equality, both legally and socially.

But the idea of erasing the antithesis between queer and straight is very threatening to many lesbians and gay men. They have become rather too attached to their gay identity. It defines their whole being. Providing more than a mere sexual orientation, it nowadays offers a complete, ready-made alternative lifestyle to those cut adrift from heterosexuality and traditional family life. There is no need for anyone attracted to people of the same sex to feel lost and uncertain. Identification with being gay gives cosy reassurance, defining a sense of personhood, place and purpose. Uncomplicated and unchallenging, it offers a mental refuge from the unpredictable sexual ambiguities and vagaries of the real world where homo and hetero desires so often coincide and intermingle. For some, gay identity has become a sexual security blanket which is clutched tight at all times. Its loss would undermine the core of their being. They cling tenaciously to a sense of gayness, with all its connotations of invariable sexual difference, certainty and exclusivity. Anything that clouds the distinctions between straight and gay is deemed suspect and dangerous. Hence the frequent irrational hostility to bisexuality and bisexuals. Lesbians and gay men with this mind-set are wedded to gay identity, not gay liberation. Happy with their homo niche in the straight world, they don't want to disturb the status quo and jeopardize their increasingly comfortable allotted sexual and social space by acknowledging other possibilities. After all, their identity as gay people gives them the security of a stable, unchanging sexual orientation.

This particular form of gay identity is implicitly committed to the preservation of sexual difference and to solidity of the gay/straight dichotomy. Because there is so much emotional investment in being gay, there is a concomitant, often unconscious, resistance to resolving the division between homos and heteros and, even more so, an unwillingness to admit the possibility that homosexuality, in the form we presently know it, might one day cease to endure.

When gay identity manifests itself in this manner, the end result is almost always a reformist gay rights agenda. Those who feel safe and satisfied with the idea of a predetermined, timeless and exclusive gayness are inevitably reluctant to rock the system that gives them such reassurance. They seek equal treatment within the social framework that heterosexuals have already established, and nothing else. Since the existing forms of homosexuality are taken for granted as eternal, and the minority status of homosexuality in society is unquestioned, there is no desire to doubt, let alone challenge, the system that sustains things as they are.

Most lesbians and gay men, if they ever had any vision of sexual emancipation, have long ago lost it. The idealism of the immediate post-Stonewall lesbian and gay liberation movement has been swamped by a short-sighted, short-termist *realpolitik*. Few homos aspire to anything more than assimilating into the hetero status quo. They happily conform to the straight system. The battle cry is gay rights, not queer emancipation. There is a big difference between the gay rights orthodoxy and the new radicalism which has been associated with contemporary queer activism and politics. The gay rights agenda focuses on the limited goal of equality, which involves parity with heterosexuals within a social structure and moral framework which straights have devised and which they dominate. In other words, equal rights on straight terms.

Those who advocate gay rights alone, without any deeper commitment to the transformation of sexuality, are concerned only with removing homophobic discrimination. They want to reform society, not fundamentally change it. Their insistence on nothing more than equal rights for queers, and their typical view of lesbians and gay men as a distinct class of people who are destined to remain forever a sexual minority separate from the straight majority, have the effect of reinforcing the divisions between hetero and homo. It encourages the false essentialist idea that gay and straight are two preordained, irreconcilable sexual orientations characteristic of two totally different types of people. Such attitudes preserve society as it is, inhibiting the movement for greater sexual choice and freedom.

While the conservative gay rights agenda is restricted to law reform to win equal rights, the more visionary queer emancipation project seeks a far-reaching sexual revolution to transform sexuality in ways that ultimately benefit both homosexuals *and heterosexuals*. It has an agenda beyond equality. Instead of merely securing equality within the pre-existing parameters of straight society, there is the more radical aim of a broader sexual liberation that expands erotic boundaries in sex-positive directions, such as the reduction of the age of consent to fourteen for everyone, the repeal of the puritanical laws against prostitution and pornography, and the introduction of explicit sex education in schools from primary classes onwards. Thus, as well as undermining heterosexual hegemony, the queer emancipation project sets its sights on subverting the whole sexphobic nature of contemporary culture. By so doing, it contributes to the diminution of all erotic guilt and repression, gay and straight.

Moderate, accommodationist gay rights politics is, ironically, solely concerned with winning rights for homosexuals. It offers nothing to heterosexual people. Whereas strident, anti-assimilationist queer activists seek the extension of sexual freedom in ways that ultimately benefit *everyone*. The radical queer activists who are so often derided as separatists are, on the contrary, the proponents of a form of sexual liberation that is, in the end, more in tune with the common interests of gays, straights and bisexuals than any purely gay rights agenda could ever be.

Should that come as a surprise? If everyone is born with the potential to be queer, as the evidence suggests, then the struggle for queer freedom is obviously in everyone's interest and we should all be working for that freedom side by side, regardless of our sexuality or gender.

Given that each of us have hetero and homo potentialities within us, the straight versus gay conflict is destructive and futile. It is a declaration of war not only against the 'other', but also against part of the self that embodies, often in repressed form, the 'otherness' we purport to reject and despise. Maintaining a 'them-and-us' antagonism simply doesn't make sense when it is so clearly in the mutual interest of queers and straights to move beyond the artificial and constricting divisions that centuries of homophobia and puritanism have imposed upon us all.

Heterosexuals are the ones who initiated the them-and-us conflict, and who continue to perpetuate it with their enforcement of homophobic intolerance. They see a very important difference between themselves and ourselves. Because of that difference, straight people claim a privileged social status, robbing queers of dignity and equality. The contrasting moral values and social rights ascribed to the differences between hetero and homo are what sustains straight supremacism. Our queer interests therefore lie in undermining the them-and-us mentality and breaking down the differences that straights use to justify our unequal treatment.

That, then, is the ultimate aspiration. The here and now practical need is often something else. So long as straight people refuse to curb their homophobia, and continue to incite tension between diverse sexualities, no one should be surprised that lesbians and gay men respond by defending 'us' against 'them'. When having a different sexual orientation is the basis for the denial of rights, queers will always need to defend their right to be different. We must insist, in the face of bigotry, that difference is not a legitimate reason for treatment as inferiors.

This defiant affirmation of sexual diversity is necessary in the short term, even if it contradicts the long-term objective of breaking down barriers. When queers are under attack, queers have a right to self-defence. Although the immediate effect of rebelling against straight hegemony is to heighten the them-and-us polarization, the eventual consequence of securing queer human rights is to subvert that polarity by eroding the heterosexism that is the ideological cement of the straight/gay division. Surprisingly, it is the assertion of the right to sexual difference that creates the conditions for the dissolution of homophobia and the evolution of a new eroticism that transgresses the boundaries of traditional heterosexuality and homosexuality.

Within the lesbian and gay community, there is enormous resistance to the idea that sexuality can and should change. The dominant 'born gay' argument, with its premise of innate and fundamental biological differences between heteros and homos, presupposes that the queer/straight split is here to stay. This biological determinist explanation of queerness has recently been given a new boost by a spate of scientific research which posits the existence of gay genes and gay brains. Unfortunately, these lacuna-riddled theories are unable to explain bisexuality or the experiences of people who, suddenly in middle age, switch from heterosexuality to homosexuality (or vice versa). What's more, the alleged differences in genetic and brain structures identified by the studies could be entirely incidental and irrelevant to the origins of homosexuality. They might just as easily be a mere correlate of sexual orientation rather than the cause.

Despite obvious theoretical and empirical weaknesses, the claims that certain genes and brain structures cause homosexuality have been seized upon and vigorously promoted by much of the lesbian and gay movement. The haste with which these unproven, questionable theories have been embraced is suggestive of a terrible lack of self-confidence and a rather sad, desperate need to justify queer desire.

The corollary of the 'born gay' idea is that no one can be 'made gay'. This defensive argument was repeatedly employed by lesbians and gay leaders during the campaign against Section 28 of the 1988 Local Government Act, which bans the 'promotion' of homosexuality by local councils. It was also resurrected during the lobbying of Parliament for the equalization of the age of consent in 1994.

At one level this is correct. Sexual orientation appears to be shaped, and become fairly fixed, in the first few years of life. For most of us it is very difficult, if not impossible, subsequently to change our sexual orientation. However, what we certainly *can* change in later life is our willingness to accept and express formerly repressed sexual desires. It *is* possible to make latent blatant.

The homophobes are, paradoxically, closer to the truth than many gay activists. Removing the social opprobrium and penalties from queer relationships, and affirming gay love and lust, would allow more people to come to terms with presently inhibited homoerotic feelings. In this sense, it is perfectly feasible to 'promote' lesbian and gay sexuality and 'make' someone queer. Individuals who have a homosexual component in their character, but are disabled by repression or guilt, definitely *can* be encouraged to acknowledge their same-sex attraction and act upon it. It stands to reason that with less homophobia there would be more homosexuality. By removing the social pressure to repress attraction to others of the same sex, many more people would feel comfortable discovering and exploring queer feelings.

Contrary to what most gay rights campaigners claim, homophobia is not irrational. It's very logical. Homosexuality is attractive and that's why it has to be ridiculed, condemned and victimized. If queer sex were really unnatural and revolting, it wouldn't have to be denigrated and suppressed by the combined forces of Parliament, police, press, pulpit and prison. There would be no need for heterosexuals to trumpet their supposed normality and superiority, no reason for them to proselytize on behalf of their straight way of life, and no justification for abrogating to themselves the exclusive legal right to marriage and financial incentives for parenthood.

Indeed, to judge by the huge resources invested by society in the promotion of heterosexuality, one might be forgiven the conclusion that it is a rather dire, unattractive option, only to be sustained by endowing itself with privileges and by the handicapping of homosexuality with a mill-stone of disparagement and disadvantage. The hysteria against homosexuality is, surely, a tacit acknowledgement of the pervasive appeal of queerness and the precarious nature of exclusive heterosexuality.

All this leads to the conclusion that if society ended its

51

favouritism towards straightness and its chastisement of gayness, same-sex desire, since it is an intrinsic human potentiality, would be much more commonplace. Sadly for queer chauvinists, this doesn't necessarily mean that more people would be lesbian and gay. In all likelihood, bisexuality would become the norm. The prevalence of both exclusive heterosexuality and exclusive homosexuality would diminish.

This poses a major challenge to those who cling to the notion of a fixed, everlasting gay identity. If sexual differentiation breaks down and hitherto distinct orientations become blurred, then the labels queer and straight lose their meaning and relevance. What is the point of striving to maintain a sense of being homosexual when the concept of a separate homosexuality is destined for extinction?

Gay identity certainly has had its historical value as a defence against compulsory heterosexuality. However, it is a passing phenomenon specific to the needs of a persecuted sexual minority in repressive societies. Once straight privilege and homophobia disappear, the need to assert a distinctive gayness will decline. Strategies for queer liberation must look to future possibilities and not be imprisoned in the limitations of the past.

The questioning of sexual categories has a subversive flip-side that is rarely discussed by queers because of the importance attached to gay identity and the fear of undermining it: if everyone is born with the potential to be attracted to the same sex, then everyone equally comes into this world with the potential to be attracted to the opposite sex. That is the rubicon the lesbian and gay movement has yet to cross. Many of us love to say that inside every straight there is a queer bursting to come out. Few are prepared to admit that inside every lesbian and gay man there might be an element of repressed straightness. To admit this does not devalue same-sex attraction or collude with homophobia. It simply concedes the liberating truth that sexuality can embody multiple, competing passions.

The possibility of one day transcending the chasm between sexual orientations is not as fanciful as some imagine. After all, the differences between gay and straight sex are, in certain respects, rather negligible.

William Masters and Virginia Johnson highlighted this in their pioneering study, *Homosexuality In Perspective* (1979). Fourteen years of clinical research led them to conclude that at the level of psychosexual functioning 'homosexuality and heterosexuality have far more similarities than differences . . . The physical capacities of erection and lubrication and the inherent facility for orgasmic attainment . . . function in identical ways, whether we are interacting heterosexuality or homosexuality. When a man or woman is orgasmic, he or she is responding to sexual stimuli in the same basic physiologic response patterns . . . regardless of whether the sexual partner is of the same or the opposite gender'.

Whatever the precise outcome of the future cultural meta-morphosis of sexuality, it is totally implausible that homo-sexuality and heterosexuality will always stay the way they are now. What will transform human sexuality more radically than anything else in the foreseeable future is the process of winning lesbian, gay and bisexual freedom. Overturning homophobia ends the need for heterosexual oppressors and homosexual victims, and subverts the whole rationale for the historic division between straight and gay.

The more we succeed in asserting our human rights as homosexuals, the sooner the differences between heteros and queers lose their significance. With no relevance or importance, the differences no longer have to be policed. Sexual boundaries become fuzzier. The need, and desire, to label behaviour and people disappears. The end result of this erosion of sexual difference will be the demise of distinct homosexual and heterosexual orientations and identities.

We queers are, it seems, destined to be the agents of both our salvation, and our supersession. By the act of gay emancipation, we sow the seeds of gay destruction. This, then, is the great paradox: queer liberation eradicates queers.

Chapter Five

FORBIDDEN FRUIT
Lisa Power

There are any amount of gay history books around these days; we've read masses about the complexities of our past heroes and heroines, we've even constructed college courses around them. Gay academia endlessly discusses the differing constructions of sexuality in different societies and centuries and now that we've celebrated the twenty-fifth anniversary of the Stonewall riots and (for those of us less US supremacist) the fortieth and fiftieth anniversaries of some of the Scandinavian and Dutch organizations, we ought to have some sense of historical continuity and diversity.

So how come we still act like things are totally different here in the late twentieth century? How come suddenly, unlike every other era, there's a gay or lesbian and there's straight and never the twain shall meet? Do we really believe that once the scales of heterosexist oppression have fallen from our eyes, we are all saved and pure, born again homosexuals? Why, despite a constant ebb and flow of people into and out of the state of grace that is currently defined as homosexuality, do we still believe in fairies for ever and ever till death us do part? Why is it still an item of scandal and surprise in most gay quarters when people behave as they always have and always will?

There has been some discussion of this issue, but only in the guise of true-life confessions in gay tabloids (followed usually by recriminations, denunciations and accusations in the letters columns) or as semi-medical discussion in lesbian AIDS leaflets, where they can be cheerfully ignored – it's not an issue widely raised in gay men's safer-sex leaflets and training. It is hard to find an even tone outside the medical or statistical reports, probably because it only arises once it has become an issue of conflict. And there is an inherent conflict within the public discussion of it. For me, it's my absolute belief that such information ought not to be a source of either surprise or shame struggling with my knowledge of the pain that other people are capable of inflicting on those who raise the issue in anything other than a theoretical sense. Yes, I think that people ought to be happy and able to tell the absolute truth about their sex lives and no, I don't think that it's anybody else's damn business, all at the same time.

But given that, in my time at least, the purpose of coming out was to be able not to live a lie; the purpose of coming to terms with one's (homo)sexuality was to be able to be comfortable with oneself and the world; the purpose of being public was to destroy the unwarranted assumptions and stereotypes of others, I am heartsick of the difficulties that most lesbian and gay communities, social groups, organizations and friendship networks have with sexuality. And of the lengths to which some people within those frameworks feel they have to go to conceal part of what should be a source of pleasure or at least amusement to them. Specifically, I mean the difficulties they have with polymorphous perversity, or open sexuality, or the ability to speak more than just your native tongue in sexual language.

Bisexuality is only the tip of it, where at least there is a certainty in the uncertainty, a clarification of the issue at stake and the difference perceived. In my experience, the real venom is reserved for those of us who just can't seem to behave according to any nice simple code of conduct; those of us who force our fellow homosexuals to understand that they are constantly living with uncertainty and shifting boundaries; that dreadful venal character, the lesbian or gay man whose lack of prejudice against the opposite sex extends occasionally to the bedroom, but who still insists on keeping their primary identifying label without shame.

To put it plainly, I am sick of lesbian and gay people, especially those involved in political or social activism, who act as a photographic negative of the heterosexual society from which they have escaped and who persecute those who do not adhere to the rigid sexual boundaries and rules they, in their turn, prescribe. I am sick of seeing honesty punished and deception and repression rewarded. I am sick of seeing people who feel forced to censor themselves or to live in two separate worlds. I am sick of seeing people who really don't like themselves because they have swallowed the lie that their personal complexities and idiosyncrasies make them Not A Real Lesbian/Gay Man, or at least a second-class one. And, of course, the reason that it makes me quite as mad as it does is because of the personal nerve that it hits. Yes, reader, (this is the true confessions bit), that Not Real Lesbian is me.

I realize that by talking about this I am a self-publicist. I am rubbing people's noses in it. I am undoubtedly an exhibitionist who gets a kick out of forcing people to discuss the revolting details of my sexual habits. Perhaps I am even advertising for like-minded sickos to indulge my perversions with, though I would have thought *Time Out* classifieds were more effective than this book and orgasms more easily achievable from writing porn, which is also better paid. I plead guilty to rubbing your noses in it, because it is about bloody time I did.

As for being a self-publicist, I fear that my reputation, at least at grass-roots level, goes before me. Although I have in fact slept with only one (gay) man in more than a decade, I have long had relayed back to me the rumours that I am Not A Real Lesbian. They emanate remarkably often from people I know to have a similar or more complex track record themselves, but let's not get into that. I receive frequent reports at approximately two- to three-month intervals about one woman who shall be nameless (I confess that's my peculiar form of revenge), who strikes up conversations with lesbians and gay men she's never met before, asks them if they've heard of me and then proceeds to denounce me for my perversions. Considering how often the stories come back, she must make a regular habit of it; the in-your-face version of the compulsive poison pen letter-writer.

Given that I have been involved with many different lesbian and gay organizations over the years, I hope that you will forgive my discretion (or possibly teasing) in not naming those where I have encountered problems because of this. I hope that they have changed or will change. I wouldn't want to insult the friendly and sensible people to be found in every one of them. I would like to see them change through their own growing awareness and not through this particular version of 'outing'. In any case, while these are stories of what happened to me, I know from others that they could have happened anywhere in the lesbian and gay activist and social movement of the 1980s and 1990s. The tales are personal, the experience universal.

The first thing that seems to happen when some people discover that you are a bit more complicated than they expect a lesbian or gay man to be is that they happily re-categorize you, usually without consulting you, as 'gone bisexual'. This is merely tedious in most organizations, but can actively damage your membership in fundamentalist ones that demand you be lesbian or gay, full stop. There have been two concerted attempts to throw me out of one such organization over the years. The first foundered from total lack of evidence of my Not a Real Lesbian status – I was just too damn friendly with the boys for some women's comfort. The second, when I cheerfully admitted the offence but pointed out that I did not wish to redefine as bisexual and asked, if they were to expel me, how long it would take to get my certificate of purity back, foundered on a mixture of confusion and genuine decency. Not, though, before it had led to a packed general meeting of the members where the personal emotional and sexual lives of myself and another had been dissected and hung out to dry to examine their possible effect upon the ability of the group to perform its mission: to support the homosexual community and promote understanding of sexuality. I will forever love the other party involved for turning up to that meeting dressed from head to foot in bright red and introducing himself in ringing tones as 'X – scarlet woman'!

The editor of a gay paper rang me casually to ask whether I would mind him mentioning that meeting and both our names in a news item for his publication; I remember how sick I felt because I was too proud to tell him not to publish but I knew that it would ruin my friendship and my membership and how relieved I was when he came to his basically decent sense on his own and left it out. The co-director of another group who heard the stories about me was really quite put out when I told him that no, it didn't mean he could claim they had a bisexual member, not unless he wanted to come out as such himself. Then there are the people with whom I've taken the time to answer their questions in as detailed a manner as was consistent with basic taste, only to watch them turn around and label me as if they'd never heard a word.

Perhaps you're one of those who think that this is a non-issue because it's such an unusual occurrence. Perhaps you're like the gay man who told me, 'None of the lesbians I know have slept with men – if they did, it would be with me. So they can't have'. Perhaps you feel sorry for me as a real oddity but can't think that this is related to ordinary lesbian or gay lives. So just let me briefly point out (this is the statistical bit, so those already convinced are welcome to skip) that an inordinate number of sexual surveys keep coming up with interesting results in this area. Sigma Research, whose reputation for scrupulous accuracy in such matters is unrivalled, found that just under 12 per cent of one sample of gay men had had sex with a woman in the past year (*Sex, Gay Men & Aids: Parameters of Sexual Behaviour*, Falmer Press 1992) and 7 per cent of their survey sample at Pride 1993 had done so (*Gay Men's Sex Survey at Pride 93*: Sigma Research and GMFA, 1993). A London magazine survey of lesbians found that approximately one in ten had slept with a man in the previous year (*City Limits,* 1992). Joyce Hunter's surveys of lesbians in the US and Rosario Iardino's in Italy come up with similar information. Within our own field, we are a minority of about the same order as homosexuals are within the wider population. And, as we so often say about those surveys, that's only the ones who've got the nerve to tell the truth.

It would not matter quite so much, perhaps, if it were not such a health hazard. We all know by now that sexual diseases spread easiest where people are disempowered from demanding safer sex. If you can't acknowledge to yourself or your partner what you are doing – the good old was-I-drunk-last-night? syndrome – it's a lot harder calculatingly to remember that condom or to tailor your acts to those suitable for safety. So when a lesbian or a gay man sleeps outside their, what shall we say?, peer group, they are less likely to remember to be safe. And with whom are they not remembering to be safe, in all likelihood? The odds are, in those surveys that remembered to ask, that it is with a homosexual of the opposite gender. It is a constant source of wonder and amazement to me to read leaflets about lesbians and AIDS that talk for pages about dental dams and gloves and just about manage to mention somewhere in the small print the shameful possibility of sexual congress with a man, pointing out of course that this might be an economically or physically forced act. In my opinion, such leaflets are active promoters of infection unless they tell the truth – that the biggest infection route for lesbians is needle sharing and the second, ashamed or was-I-drunk-last-night? and therefore unprotected sex with gay and other men.

And of course, it is that risk that gets translated as one of the other big fears, expressed inelegantly to my face at an academic conference on homosexuality: that you never know what she's got, do you, if she's been with one of those dirty men. I would have thought that this was a reason to promote sexual health checks rather than to try and fly in the face of nature, but perhaps political lesbian feminist separatists have had more practice at the latter than I have. I remember vividly a lesbian who had made it abundantly clear that she was after my body on at least a short-term hire arrangement, with whom I simply tried to raise the general issue of safer sex and what, if anything, it might mean to us. Had I, she enquired faintly, any reason for asking, like, had I been doing it with gay men? Er, well, I stuttered, one of them, once only recently (which was at that moment true), but utterly, totally, safely – honest. I didn't even think of daring to ask her the same in return. She kissed me warmly on the cheek and helped me make up the spare bed.

But lesbians have been no worse, in their particularly upfront way, in dealing with this issue than gay men. At least lesbian sexual health materials mostly mention men in some way; the overwhelming majority of gay men's material pretends, like large chunks of the 1980s gay scene did, that women don't exist at all, let alone get fucked by faggots. Peter Tatchell's important safer-sex manual launched by Freedom Editions in 1994, while using throughout the politically up-to-date buzz phrase 'gay and bisexual men', went on to pretend that every sexual act they needed to consider only and always involved men, including group sex. The vast number of 'comprehensive' safer-sex tracts for gay men spend pages of text lovingly describing and often lavishly illustrating activities undertaken by statistically far fewer gay men than those having sex with women.

The first line of defence on this is that there are plenty of leaflets around about safer heterosexual sex; but what gay man careful of his image would be seen dead reading one, and if it's that easy, what's the point of all this lavish targeting of leaflets to specific population groups? And where do any of those leaflets deal with the guilt and awkwardness of sexual negotiation with someone outside your usual and accepted object of choice? I once watched a founder member of a leading UK organization on gay men and AIDS being challenged about why their acclaimed training, given the above facts, never ever mentioned women. He had no coherent answer. 'The simple fact is', a close associate of theirs told me quietly in the next meeting break, 'they're afraid that they'd get laughed at'. Where lesbians condemn you, gay men just laugh you out of court.

It's not just the unpleasant effects of such foolishness on the individual. There's no doubt that over the past twenty-five years the lesbian and gay movement has hardened; as our identity is strengthened, so it also becomes more exclusive and large enough to shelter people from the messy realities of the outside world. We have gone from a rag tag collection of liberationists and people in nice sweaters in bars to being a lifestyle and a market and our identity is no longer that of difference but of merely a different sameness – as the Scarlet Woman puts it, from PC to PLC. 'If you can love men, you can't love women' (a very young lesbian separatist said to me last year) echoes 'Four legs good, two legs bad'. I have never managed to convince myself that to love each other we must learn to hate everyone else and I doubt that I will ever learn to turn my affections into a company limited by guarantee for anyone.

So, what's to do? My behaviour (I mean the telling, not the doing) is anathema to some lesbians and gay men, who wish that people like me would either shut up or go somewhere else. I admit that when I was the elected figurehead of an international lesbian and gay federation, I had some sympathy with the fellow committee member who said gently that he thought it might be a little tactless of me to make any public announcement of my recent adventure while still in post. And yet, I know from personal discussions that I wasn't the only person elected to that position who had made that sort of sexual choice – and, of course, agreed or decided to keep to the simplified version of our reality so as not to upset the apple cart of the membership.

The thing is, you see, we're like a secret society within you. We're everywhere and we know who each other is. We talk about it behind your backs. I've seen us pick each other up under your noses, I've even pointed it out only to be totally disbelieved (next time, I'm betting money). But mostly we keep schtum to you, because you wouldn't understand and you might pick on us. Does it sound familiar?

Please don't think I'm trying to be a martyr. I've never felt less like one in my life, since a couple of years ago when I finally lost my temper with a woman who was trying to get me to accede to relocating a lesbian meeting to another venue – any other venue – than my home, because of my 'controversial attitude'. It was the nearest she could get to saying 'because you've fucked a gay man and you might infect someone else with the same idea, if nothing else'. I shouted at her for some time down a phone while my best lesbian friend held my hand and the man in question made me coffee and then I went back into an office we all shared and wrote down exactly what I thought of the whisper campaign for them all to read. And told them that if they didn't like it, it was their problem. I've felt just wonderful about it ever since. And any trouble I have had over my tiny transgressions has been as nothing compared to what more public personalities like Tom Robinson, the singer, and Christopher Spence, the founder of London Lighthouse, have faced for being unrepentantly self-identified gay men while living in blissfully happy long-term domestic relationships with women.

I suppose I could run away and join the bisexuals and believe me, there are a few people who have suggested it, some more kindly than others. Some people do, if they like that sort of thing. The bisexual movement just now is a bit like the early gay movement at the same stage. That is, a high proportion of unrealistic optimism and energy and a big ration of total loonies. There are many people within it that I admire, respect and even love but I don't see the point of yet another subdivision of the movement. I agree with bisexual friends about the need for honesty about who you are and what you do; but if, as I'm always being told, my lesbian identity is wider than just what I do in bed, then I will resist the contraction of the label to exclude me. I didn't suspend my membership of the lesbian nation for a few weeks while I had a holiday in heteroland. And if refusing the label of bisexual is, as some bi-supremacists suggest, a cop-out then why make such a clear commitment to neither lying nor hiding the relationship? I know what I prefer, and the bisexual politic seems to me to be a reaction to the exclusions of gay, whereas gay has always been so much more than just a reaction to the exclusions of straight. There's nothing wrong with it for those who want to use it as their label but, like frilly satin frocks, it just doesn't suit me no matter which way I do my hair.

I could do what an increasing number of activists, particularly cultural activists and journalists, seem to have taken to doing and renounce my membership of the lesbian and gay movement on the grounds that I'm Too Big For It. I could run around, having made my reputation and my early crust from my homosexuality and my attachment to it, and write articles for the straight press denouncing my former stunted, sad life in the ghetto and helping heterosexuals to feel smug. Except that I can't help but feel that such temper tantrums are much more a sign that people are too small than that they are too big; that in their perfectly reasonable desire to transgress, their devotion to deviancy, they have mistaken homosexuality for a powerful State against which they must rail. When people publicly leave something and then have to spend a lot of time attacking it, I often think that somehow the leaving cannot have been entirely their own choice, or at least not a decision that has made them happy. I could become queer, except that it is so desperately early 90s, darling, or I could become post-queer except that like a bad dream I can only remember what it means when I'm standing in the foyer of London's ICA Gallery. I could become a straight woman who generally prefers to sleep with other women, but I've known that and it's not a pretty fate.

The trouble is, I don't feel like going anywhere else. There are plenty of sensible people in the lesbian and gay movement; despite anything else, I've never felt so supported in my life. The movement can't stand still, or like anything else organic it would die. There will never be a total defeat of ignorance and prejudice, any more than we can totally erase homophobia; some people will always only be able to live with themselves by constructing ways of feeling superior to others. But it's possible to shift the emphasis so that peer consensus is more liberal than censorious, more enlightened than uniform. Humanity is a state of change and exploration, a cradle for us to make of ourselves whatever we can and whatever we wish. That's also what my lesbian and gay movement is. I'm not leaving any movement; people in it might choose to leave me but, as I've said on a number of occasions since I first said it to my fellow members of that previously mentioned organization, that's their problem and not mine. Anti-gay? I don't think so.

Chapter Six

INDIGESTION:
DIAGNOSING THE GAY MALADY
Jo Eadie

It is always interesting for me, as a bisexual man, to hear what the
lesbian and gay community is saying about bisexuality. Indeed, it is
something that bisexual people in general put a lot of energy into.
Maybe this is why we seem to be regarded as a bunch of gay
wannabes – maybe we think about it too much to ever really get
away from it. Still, I go on listening, and thinking about it. One of
the latest twists in this whole eavesdropping process came from
lesbian photographer Della Grace on Channel 4's *Without Walls*
programme 'Lesbians Unclothed'. She said: 'If a lesbian sleeps with
a man she's not bisexual, she's adventurous'. That remark makes a
bid to exclude bisexuality at any price. Better, it would seem, to
stretch the term 'lesbian' to the point of incoherence, than to
recognize bisexuality in its own right. Better that a woman, even if
she decides never to sleep with women again, do anything rather
than call herself bisexual. Grace offered this, curiously enough, as an
example of the increasing tolerance of the lesbian community.

The question I was prompted to ask is: does Grace want this
woman or not? She seems to be doing her best to retain her, but at
the same time doesn't want to ask *her* who *she* thinks she is. And,
intrigued by that, I set about tracing just what it is that the lesbian
and gay community wants from us bisexuals. Does it want us, or
not? Does it want us to do anything, as long as we don't use the b-
word? Why is that so important to them? What I'll be documenting
here are the convolutions that lesbians and gay men put themselves

through in order to preserve the integrity of their world. And at the same time, the discomfort, which I liken to indigestion, that results from the trace of a desire for bisexual people which threatens – or perhaps promises – to break that world apart.

I THINK YOU LOVE ME . . .

Here is Rose Collis in *Gay Times* (March 1994) reviewing the documentary *Sandra Bernhard – Confessions of a Pretty Lady*. After a generally enthusiastic account she concludes:

> However Bernhard says she doesn't really see herself as an idol for dykes, but more for straight women for whom the word 'sexuality' could be the name of a new perfume. 'I'm a spokesperson for the modern woman' she declares – and an old quote about idols with feet of clay comes to mind.

So Bernhard is a failure as a lesbian idol. What is so odd about this passage is that Bernhard is being accused of failure in the very same paragraph where Collis refers to Bernhard's denial that she wants to be an idol. 'An idol with feet of clay' – maybe, but who was it who made her 'an idol for dykes'? Who set her up as what she wasn't and then was disappointed when she failed? What seems to be at issue here is that insofar as Bernhard has spoken of, and acted upon, and incorporated into her performance, sexual desire for women, she must, it follows, be a lesbian.

We can see exactly the same argument in Elspeth Probyn's reading of Bernhard in her book *Sexing The Self* (Routledge, 1993). In what is otherwise one of the most perceptive and sophisticated accounts of Bernhard's film *Without You I'm Nothing* (1990), Probyn laments:

> And yet, one of the obvious things the film forgets to mention is lesbian desire. For all her right-on rhetoric, Sandra never says anything directly about wanting the black woman [in the audience of

67

her show], or for that matter any woman at all. Sure, she turns 'Me and Mrs Jones' against itself into a lesbian torch song . . . but, in actual fact, in actual words, she never quite comes out.

So she won't quite fit, she's not lesbian enough, she's not a complete, a real, an authentic lesbian. And yet twelve pages earlier Probyn says it clearly enough:

> While Madonna has never quite come out, Sandra repeatedly does so in various ways that don't quite conform to the dictates of gay and lesbian pride: as bi-sexual [sic], as involved with a man, as sleeping with different women, etc.

Putting Collis and Probyn together I was struck that each begins with rhetorical gesture of reversal: Collis' 'however', Probyn's 'and yet' – strategic ways of retracting the praise that has led up to these final, very similar, denunciations. The recognition of Bernhard's performance of a dissident bisexuality, which will never conform to the dictates, and which Probyn even goes so far as to name, ends up being turned against her as 'she never quite comes out' (i.e. as a lesbian). If you don't do the *right* thing, you haven't done anything. The evidence of her success is marshalled as the evidence of her failure: because she went so far, asserted a certain recognizable lesbian image, she should have followed it through to a conclusion, but she didn't – what a disappointment.

What we are up against here is a form of attention which can in fact only perceive us (us bisexuals) as lesbian, or as gay. That might, for some, be a positive political change, because there was a time when we were all assumed to be straight. But now we are left with a situation where when we don't make ourselves visible in those terms we are deficient, blamed in terms familiar to any straight woman: she led me on, she must have meant it, she looked like she was offering it, she let me down.

And it is that similarity to the straight male language of being 'led on' which might suggest that this blindness is more than just a form of attention – it is a structure of desire. The caption for Collis' review – picking up from the Eighth London Lesbian and Gay Film Festival's title 'Wild Things' – is 'I think I love you . . . '. And there on the page next to it is Bernhard's picture with Collis' quote, this time with a question mark added to it: 'feet of clay?'. Those prevarications mark the ambiguity of these texts, and of their writers' feelings: Bernhard has enough of the signs to be wanted, to look lesbian, for Collis and Probyn to want her in with them, and to want her – but somehow their desire wavers, turned aside because it does not encounter the object that it hoped for. So is it 'those bisexuals' who are so very ambiguous, or isn't it rather those who look on us, who can't decide?

Elsewhere in the same issue of *Gay Times* we find Joseph Mills writing on gay idols who aren't gay enough. Some of it is an appropriate attack on men who have benefited from a gay following and since made homophobic remarks – Mel Gibson, Marky Mark. Some of it, reading much like Collis' piece, is a diatribe against those who are so cute they ought to be gay and have let us down by being heterosexual – or even worse, by losing their good looks. 'Can you forgive them?' it is titled – again, a question mark, and again, the blame cast on the objects of the enquiry: shifting the emphasis away, conveniently, from the ambiguous desires of the audience. Maybe these lesbian and gay equivocations should be collected under the banner 'we can't make up our minds'. Or even 'we're sitting on the fence'.

Perhaps the most distasteful moment is in Mills' dismissal of Tom Robinson – fairly out and political about his bisexuality you might have thought. You are wrong:

> Tom Robinson went from foremost gay rights lecturer to a hetero relationship and fatherhood . . . Would Tom Robinson have investigated a relationship with a female if (a) he could have children

with a man (b) homosexuality was the norm and what his parents
wanted of him.

Fundamental to this is the implicit misogyny in the assumption that
no bisexual man would have a relationship with 'a female' were it
not for the possibility of parenthood. Mills responds with horrified
disbelief at the thought that anyone could think of leaving behind
homosexuality, that anyone could want anything else. On the one
hand he is insisting that you don't count unless you live that life
fully, on the other hand he obviously wants these people to stand up
and be counted. But by his logic, they never can be counted, they can
only be *dis*counted because they are unrecognizable – for we are
back to the impossibility of recognizing bisexuality as such. It can
only be seen as a failed imitation of true homosexuality. And it is
expected to display all the requisite codes of that great figure which
haunts the sexual imagination since the late nineteenth century – the
homosexual, here required to stand up, as visible, as conforming, as
recognizable as Wilde on trial.

But whereas for the heterosexual imagination, the figure of the
homosexual must be brought forth in order to be rejected, for the
lesbian and gay imagination it must be brought forth in order to be
assimilated. Those who look this way, talk this way, act this way,
must belong: look at how they dress, they're asking for it. Mills'
register conflates a personal desire – for these men, physically,
sexually – with a political desire: that these men be part of the
lesbian and gay movement.

This is an interesting weave of desires which comes up again in
Gay Times the next month (April 1994), when Wayne Berntsen
writes in response to an interview with all-boy pop group Two
Thirds. Throughout the interview the three men remained carefully
ambiguous and suggestive about their sexuality, which earned them
the following response: 'To us knowing gays they're blatantly
obvious . . . and of course they will pretend to be straight . . . we

could do without this sort of cowardice. Be out, be proud'. We all know the signs, they can only mean one thing. So it was very gratifying, and much to the point of this essay, to find Two Thirds replying the next month (May 1994) as follows: 'What do you want to read, "we fuck men"?' Having made that old Pet Shop Boys point that it doesn't need to be said to be obvious, the band then in effect overturn that argument by stating: 'we will also tell you that two of our members also like girls. Not that old Elton claim either but genuine uncertainty of all of our sexuality'. Those apparently obvious signs never in fact secure anything. Although camp, boyish looks, and homoerotic playfulness might be indicted as too unclear, even the most blatant statement of homosexuality – 'we fuck men' – turns out not to be enough of a peg to hang a secure gay identity on. Which of course is what is at stake here: secure gay identities.

One great exemplar of that dependence on secure categories is Sheila Jeffreys. Here is one of her two passing references to bisexuality from her new book *The Lesbian Heresy* (The Women's Press, 1994), where she talks about efforts to make the London Lesbian and Gay Centre more inclusive. She frames the debate as an opposition between the inclusion of a range of sexualities (the familiar grouping of transsexuals, sadomasochists, bisexuals and paedophiles) and a pure lesbian and gay space. In her version of this drama, supporting inclusivity are gay men who 'were commited to supporting sexual minorities, seeing their own homosexuality as just one more perversion in a list of increasingly exotic sexual types'. The issues finally come down to this: 'the only choice open to lesbians who wanted to use the facilities of the centre was to accept or cease to criticise gay male sexual politics. Those who found them indigestible girlcotted the centre'. We can see in that conflict a persistent attempt to confine what it means to be lesbian or gay by demanding that those who are not quite, should conform, or get out. As if that insistence would thereby prove that the lesbian and gay community, the lesbian and gay identity, was quite adequate for anyone, if only these foolish people would realize it and change themselves so as to fit. What is so interesting about Jeffreys' fantasy of a digestible politics, is that it has so much in common with other lesbian and gay discourse on bisexuality, even those which do not seem to share her politics. In other words, the hostility towards the indigestible bisexual is not simply a consquence of Jeffreys' politics, as this passage might seem to show, but rather is a very familiar position which simply finds a new expression in her politics. Mills, Probyn and Collis all also find bisexuals indigestible.

What leads to that indigestion is not, as Jeffreys presents it, that an otherwise smoothly functioning gay digestive system has been force-fed bisexuals. Rather it is the attempts by that system to devour: their craving for us. What we are beginning to see here is that bisexuals are not simply expelled, but are pursued, sought after, solicited, cajoled. And all with the aim of getting us to fit in. So let us read the lesbian and gay relationship with bisexuality as a fundamentally hungry one: an impulse to devour, ingest and incorporate, where Sandra Bernhard's 'feet of clay' are the indigestible morsel that sticks in the throat; where the homosexual portion is savoured, while the heterosexual portion is vomited out – which for most of us, means vomited *on*. And of course, as with all indigestible food, the blame falls on us: on the way we taste, on the way we make ourselves unpalatable.

The problem lies not with the food, but with the appetite: with a body which cannot digest us, but which wants to devour us; with a gaze which thinks that we are asking for it. The particular intractability of Jeffreys' version of lesbian feminism, where 'lesbians did not see why they should accept transsexuals in the lesbian toilets since *they* did not see surgery as having made them women' (my emphasis) marks a politics without dialogue or exchange, where what does not fit into a pre-existing political imaginary has to be excluded. Any politics which looks towards openness and the erosion of fixed boundaries is figured by Jeffreys as 'a list of increasingly exotic sexual types'. Her provincial appetite conflates 'increasingly exotic' with 'indigestible': let's stick to the diet we know and love, none of this foreign muck on *our* plates.

As is so often the case with cultural anxieties about diet, what hides underneath it is seduction: that the indigestible might perhaps be assimilated, that in time the devourer might get a taste for it. While Jeffreys may want a whole range of sexual dissidents excluded from the digestive economy, she is also, like Mills and Collis and Probyn, just a bit hungry for the bisexual woman, who is significantly absent. The term 'bisexual' only ever seems to apply to bisexual men in her story. That visible absence from Jeffreys' equation and from her justification for the exclusion of bisexuals is necessary precisely because the bisexual woman would confuse that act of sharp differentiation and rejection by introducing desire, in the form of a woman-loving-woman who would seem necessary and important for – that is, wanted by – the politics of this passage.

Running implicitly through all these encounters with bisexuality is the question of wanting. The lesbian and gay community asks it with the fervour that characterizes it on demonstrations: 'What do we want?'. There are a number of possible answers, but what they all have in common is that (1) the questioner knows what the answer will be, with the certainty of a ritual liturgy, and (2) the answer basically means 'more of the same': more lesbians like the ones we have, more gay men like the ones we have, more pubs, clubs, books, magazines – much, much more please: but more of the same. Not the new, or different – that is denounced as exotic or indigestible, as faulty or deficient, for difference can only be defect. Even though these calls are legitimate political demands, they are nevertheless articulated at the expense of bisexuality. Those faces which stare from the covers of the 'pink press' are the faces of those who know who they are, and who invite us to recognize our shared identity in that proud stare. All they really need to be complete would be a version of the famous slogan from Kitchener's war recruitment poster: 'Homosexuality Needs You'.

These issues are fundamental to the two great debates of the last five years in the lesbian and gay community, over outing and queer. Like those defiant faces, the calls for outing and queer politics speak of the need for visibility, the importance of declaring a sexual difference, the right to challenge heterosexist assumptions. Where they both founder is in their return, ultimately, to just as static a notion of sexual identity as that which they were hoping to resist. Outing is predicated on the figure of the homosexual, whose true nature can be exposed – defiantly or scornfully, depending on the situation. But the assumption remains that the figure's sexuality is identical to that of the exposer, whose fixed identity can be held up to public scrutiny. So, too, queer politics offered a new, high-profile, in-your-face label. And yet it wasn't long before the original promise of an alliance across sexual diversities became a new word for 'lesbian and gay' with the same exclusions. One of the first pieces of queer literature declared: 'there are straight queers, bi-queers, tranny queers, lez queers, fag queers, SM queers, fisting queers in every single street in this apathetic country of ours'. But responding to that quotation three years on at the British Sociological Association's 1994 'Sexualities in Social Context' conference, one speaker – to general approval – dismissed it, noting with some relief that straight queers seemed to have gone the same way as feminist men. The lesbian and gay community, while interested in *challenging* current terms, remains uninterested in following this process through to its difficult conclusion, that radical change in hegemonic forms of heterosexuality and male misogyny would erode the basis for the original opposition. Far better, it would seem, to make homes in 'our' own ghettos and leave 'them' to go on ruling the world – because if they should change, then we will have to change too. If the 'straight' become queer, if 'men' become 'feminist' then, also, the premises of that politics (you're the enemy, you're nothing like us, you hate us, you want to destroy us so we'll never be like you, we need to get away from you) become rather less tenable. The narcissistic yearning for a place where 'we' only find others like ourselves, and where 'they' are nothing like 'us' comes up against its own limits. And those limits are precisely that identity does not inhere in specific persons – the lesbian, the gay man, the bisexual, the straight – but that these terms only name provisional sites which are intersected by a range of practices, desires, attitudes and politics which never come together in the same way every time.

Now might be the time to restate two, perhaps rather basic, points which tend to slip out of the debate. First, a shared identity is no guarantee of a shared commitment to a genuinely liberating project. A supposedly 'lesbian' or 'gay' – or for that matter 'bisexual' – space is quite capable of generating discourses which perpetuate the disempowerment of that group. The quest for a biological origin of homosexuality is just such an issue, with (primarily) gay male researchers happily sustaining a minoritizing position of homosexual desire, and thereby propping up the heterosexist apparatus which dismisses our desires as the fixed, and contained, sickness of a small group who can't help it.

Second, the overlap of identities and communities in which any one of us is situated means that any collective action can neglect other equally important, and damaging, regimes of power. For example, the pink economy goes on selling overpriced goods made by underpaid workers, and gay sexual tourism participates in an imperialist legacy. This is not simply to say that 'we' (lesbians, gays, bisexuals) are sustaining 'their' (the working class, the so-called 'Third World') oppression. We are also sustaining the systems which perpetuate our own oppression – in these two cases, capitalism's continued (although mutable) reliance on the family, and the West's narrow conception of sexuality which Western supremacist positions do nothing to question.

If we base our resistance around particular discourses – racism, crass biologism, rigid gender roles, body fascism – rather than insisting that those discourses are the properties of set groups, then we are as likely to be confronting power, prejudice and hostility within our communities as outside it. But then that would just be so much less comfortable. Wouldn't it? The desire to find completeness and self-sufficiency goes on making it much easier to hope for union and unity than to recognize the impossibility of that dream. Far better, it would seem, to go on being hungry – to on wanting that ideal man or woman who is in actual fact, in actual words, *just like me*.

WHAT WILL BE?

Perhaps we can draw on a bisexual image to offer a different way of expressing that hunger to get what we want. As a counterpoint to the narcissistic faces of the lesbian and gay press, I want to refer to a (suggestively faceless) image from the cover of a bisexual publication. When *Bifrost*, a British bisexual magazine, depicts a woman wearing a strap-on dildo there can be no automatically assumed target audience for a face to look at. Instead, there is a pointing penis which might be aimed at a straight man, a dyke, a bisexual man, another bisexual woman – it might even be aimed at a straight woman, or a gay man.

The appetite that I read in that bisexual image is an appetite which cannot answer that shouted question: which has not decided in advance what it wants. It is an appetite which is predicated on the very unknowability of the new, and which therefore begins to offer a way beyond indigestion. Epitomizing resistance to the new is the great gay anthem 'Que sera, sera', which opens with that radical uncertainty – will it be this? Will it be that? – and then swiftly closes it down: what will be, will be. In this bisexual questioning, however, what 'will be' could be anything.

That question of the future, is crucial in these issues of bisexuality. The desire that bisexual people fit in is a response to a very strong fear – a fear about the future, and a fear of destruction. A clear articulation of that comes through in a description by Elizabeth Wilson of why there can be no place for bisexual people within lesbian and gay politics. Throughout her explanation she is recognizing – and warding off – the haunting possibility that bisexuality will dissolve lesbian and gay identity:

> The demand for the recognition of bisexuality challenges the foundations of the lesbian and gay movement, which for better or worse, is predicated on the assumption that the lesbian/gay identity is at least relatively fixed . . . we must recognise the problems this poses for political activism, and the bisexual movement in its demand for recognition primarily from the lesbian and gay movement has been insensitive to these difficulties. —*Elizabeth Wilson*, 'Is transgression transgressive?', in *Activating Theory*, ed. Joseph Bristow and Angelia R. Wilson (Lawrence and Wishart, 1993).

What Wilson manages to ignore – and what she falsely assumes we do not care about – is the level of discussion about this issue in the bisexual community: a concern to honour the gains made under the umbrella of gay liberation and lesbian feminism, the concern not to destroy or damage the communities that exist and the needs that they meet. She neatly glosses over the terminally narrow predicates of the politics inherent in the naming of 'lesbian and gay'. Here again we find that bisexual activists' dissatisfaction at the failure of lesbian and gay politics to match up to the real lives of the queer multitude it supposedly champions is inverted so that it is our fault for not fitting in with a perfectly good agenda. The threat that bisexuality poses to lesbian and gay politics is much the same that sexuality poses to the Right's vision of the family: it makes it clear that the ideal is simply inappropriate.

What Wilson is offering, like Jeffreys, is a fantasized perfect digestive economy, where only the palatable is encountered, and it is essential to resist the recognition of difference. Difference is again blamed: this time we are 'insensitive'. What all these accusations cover over is the fact that bisexuality demands a change in the persistence with which both the political and the popular discourses of sexuality conceive of same-sex desires as solely the property of an established lesbian and gay community. A change in the assumption that anybody experiencing such desires is on their way into that community, and will remain there. And a change in the assumption that to do anything else is to be a failure.

In order to facilitate that change, I want to suggest a reading strategy. If that might remind some of the hold that cultural studies has on contemporary sexual theory, I want to mark here its location in another tradition, the tradition of the inquisitive gay and lesbian gaze which looked out for the traces and signs of homosexuality. And if, for the last few centuries, what has been enabling about that reading practice has been its capacity to recognize, across a crowded room or not-so crowded heath, a fellow traveller, it is now perhaps time to see how that gaze might be perpetuating these damaging misrecognitions.

In *S/Z*, an analysis of how a short story by Balzac offers itself to being read, Roland Barthes elaborates his notion of connotation, which is that level of meaning in a text which hovers over the apparently given, denoted meaning to produce:

> an agglomerative space, certain areas of the text correlating other meanings outside the material text and, with them, forming 'nebulae' of signifieds. Topologically, connotation makes possible a (limited) dissemination of meanings . . . Functionally, connotation, releasing

the double meaning on principle, corrupts the purity of comunication: it is a deliberate 'static'.

Purity of communication is dependant on the assumption that a fixed meaning is carried unproblematically from sender to receiver. But Barthes is pointing out an agglomeration of meanings out of which denotation 'is ultimately no more than the last of the connotations', given special privilege by reading practices directed towards closure and unity. For instance, make-up connotes effeminacy connotes sexual ambiguity, the meanings nested one inside the other. But in steps someone to stop the chain: sexual ambiguity denotes gayness.

Barthes describes this reductive process in terms resonant of homosexuality. Describing that reading practice which attempts to contain connotations by gathering them under a single 'name', he points out that 'when the unnesting of names ceases, a critical level is established, the work is closed, the language by which the semantic transformation is ended becomes nature, truth, the work's secret'. Hence we can look at the ways in which Bernhard is denoted as lesbian, but connotes her bisexuality (and at other times, vice versa); or how Tom Robinson's recent album *Lover Over Rage* connotes his gayness, although his life might be said to denote heterosexuality. In such denotative reading, Robinson's male-female relationship becomes not another mobile signifier with numerous connotations but just that last name: nature, truth, the work's secret, its mass of different meanings closed down.

For Barthes, an image is saturated with such connotations, and this is of course a key reading strategy of lesbian and gay culture, long used to recognize camp, butch/femme, or SM in unexpected places, revealed by incidental gestures, looks, words. In a similar way, Jeffreys' feminism has a history of locating the silenced but connoted resistances, angers and frustrations of women, the signs that break through the official history. But rather than holding on to the plurality that it unleashes, the knowing gaze of these knowing gays reduces that multiple connotation back to a single meaning, violating the intuition of plurality which produced it. But those connotations are proving an increasingly unstable ground for such politics, where no 'look' necessarily matches up to an assumed identity, and perhaps some of that multiplicity can find its way back in. There have been innumerable recent panics about the inadequacy of connotations as the basis for imputed sexuality. The *Pink Paper* has run an article on how to distinguish real lesbians from tourist lesbians ('my guide for weeding out . . . the wheat from the chaff' as it is described, 27 May 1994); meanwhile there is a shock that East 17 should support a gay male age of consent of twenty-one even though they look gay(ish).

That 'static', that counter-communication, is a version of the other disturbances I have elaborated – indigestion. If indigestion is the failure of the body to assimilate the different, the process by which foreignness is established, then 'static' is the process by which reception itself is problematized. It interferes with the very eating process, offering an unpalatable, because only partially recognizable, object. From this position we could read Bernhard's bisexuality not as the separable chunk that gets ejected, but as a connotative disturbance in the lesbian image which would be a preemption of, rather than merely a postscript to, her being configured as an icon.

Connotations overlay the narcissistic mirror, so that the observed figure does not simply resemble us, but rather resonates with connotations which different audiences may share. Hence we can reread Berntsen's letter about Two Thirds as the recognition by a gay reader of *some* shared connotations – but that similarity does not exhaust the connotations of these three men, nor does it require that we press those connotations into the service of a denoted homosexuality. In the original interview which provoked the letter, Richard Smith constantly comes up against a degree of similarity, but never perfect identity – hence of course their name, Two Thirds: not complete as they should be, but partly.

Perhaps the encounter with Two Thirds could, more productively, have explored what it means for people who are not, by the current rather limited definitions, 'gay', to nevertheless live, breathe and *own* those connotations, where connotation includes a politics, and a sexual practice, as well as a look.

Two Thirds operates as a suggestive figure for the love that might speak its name but can never be heard, for partial similarity rather than absolute identity. It reminds us (us bisexuals) not to make the same mistake, i.e. the mistake of asking why lesbians who have sex with men won't come out as bisexual, or lamenting that Tom Robinson goes on calling himself gay. We don't need identity in order to have solidarity. This is why connotation is so important, because it allows the circulation of similarities without foreclosing difference. Whenever Pride is reported in the lesbian and gay press, the opening line inevitably reads 'thousands of lesbians and gays', ignoring not only the bisexuals, but the straight supporters, who for the most part are indistinguishable. In the circulation of 'signs' that takes place on such an occasion, who can know what they mean? Those two men with their arms around each other – lovers, or a gay man with his straight brother? That group of shaven-headed women – a bunch of bi girls, or even a bunch of their straight friends?

What this suggests for activism is, of course, a way around that insistence by lesbians and gay men that bisexuals are 'different' in a world where everyone is *either* the Same *or* Different. If, as bisexuals, we have similar but not always identical needs, shared with lesbians and gay men (who, as groups, do not themselves have identical needs), if we are affected similarly *and* differently by legal and institutional oppressions, then perhaps we can start to evolve a politics which is not based around denoted sameness, but connoted similarities. We might respond to Sheila Jeffreys' dismissal of indigestible transsexuals by pointing out that just because a trans-sexual woman is not identical to a non-transsexual woman, that does not mean she is not *similar*.

Barthes calls for 'an infinite thematics, open to endless nomination', which is something of what that *Bifrost* cover offers. Barthes enables a way of speaking about confusion: not in the sense of the 'confused bisexual', but in the sense of an encounter with an object which confuses the viewer. Scrambled communication allows the imprecision, the multiplicity, the incoherence of the object to be received, so that what is difficult or troubling need no longer be excluded or condemned, and what is famliar and comforting need no longer be privileged.

Appetite is, by definition, not sure of what it wants – an insight which might perhaps enable the lesbian and gay community to stop reaching for what it can't have (i.e. bisexuals who act gay), and also prevent the bisexual community from heading into that same dead end.

When Joseph Mills looks back to Bowie on stage in 1973, and wants to dispute Bowie's subsequent avowed heterosexuality, he has much the same reaction as any homophobe: 'you mean that camp, painted tart in a mini-skirt simulating buggery on stage and swishing a scarlet boa round his neck was what a heterosexual looks like?'. Surely not – if he's heterosexual he *must* be wearing – what? A suit and tie maybe? Only the elect gay few are allowed to look like that.

It is not the bisexual who is deficient, but the lesbian and gay gaze in not noticing; not the bisexual who is insatiable, but lesbian and gay politics which needs to devour us; not the bisexual who is ambiguous but the lesbian and gay community which is ambivalent about its feelings; not bisexuals who say 'everyone is one of us really', but lesbians and gay men who believe all bisexuals are lesbian or gay 'really'; not we who are confused about what we want, but you; not our appetite which is so troubling, but yours.

Indigestion is at the core of the gay body politic. Its constant invitation to queers to come and join the party (in either sense of the word) results in a discomforting mass of foreign bodies lodged inside, stuck in its throat, or undigested in its stomach. The cure would be to recognize that the signs which have been collected around the figure of the homosexual – camp, music, leather, butch/femme – even the most blatant, secure signs – we fuck men – in fact secure nothing. They are only the available terms through which different identities are enabled to speak. They do not – and this is crucial because it is the very opposite of how those signs are usually read – *tell us anything.*

Chapter Seven

CONFESSIONS OF A GAY FILM CRITIC, OR HOW I LEARNED TO STOP WORRYING AND LOVE *CRUISING*

Paul Burston

The history of the portrayal of lesbians and gay men in mainstream cinema is politically indefensible and aesthetically revolting.

—*Vito Russo*[1]

When dealing with ideology it is always necessary to ask not only what it *ex*presses but what it *re*presses.

—*Robin Wood*[2]

HOW TO GO TO THE MOVIES

It's not an easy job being a gay film critic – not when you consider the enormous responsibilities involved. Ever since Vito Russo took Hollywood to task over its 'politically indefensible' and 'aesthetically revolting' portrayal of lesbians and gay men, those critics who openly identify as lesbian or gay have been encouraged to view mainstream films with the same level of suspicion he did. Ever since Robin Wood took the decision to come out and re-evaluate the films of Bergman, Hawks and Hitchcock in light of his own personal liberation, the role of gay film critic has been weighted with a responsibility to attack not only the 'negative' images of lesbians and gay men identified in specific films, but also 'the economic structures of capitalism that support the norms, as they are embodied in the structure of the film industry itself as well as in its products'.[3]

Between them, Russo and Wood took all the fun out of going to the movies.

I'm joking, of course. Being paid to write about films still rates as one of the most enjoyable jobs in the world. And one of the easiest to get away with performing badly – particularly when you happen to be gay. There was a time when I would have been inclined to take a leaf out of Richard Dyer's book and suggest that 'gays' and 'film' go together like a horse and a particularly large penis. Sadly, this isn't always the case. Turn to the film pages in any popular gay publication and you'll see that, for every lesbian or gay man who grew up delighting in the promiscuous pleasures offered by the movies, there are numerous others who never progressed beyond the desire to see themselves reflected on the big screen. In an adolescent, this fixation would be entirely understandable; in an adult, it begins to beg a few questions. Comforting as it is to be shown that, actually you are not the only homosexual in the world, a constant craving for affirmation of one's identity can hardly be a sound basis for a career as a film critic.

Traditionally, two assumptions have shaped the way in which films are reviewed in the popular gay press. The first – that films made *by* gay people *for* gay people are somehow above criticism – is, thankfully, going out of fashion. Years of sitting through the most appalling rubbish, and feeling obliged to applaud the film-maker's efforts, have clearly taken their toll, even on those clap-happy viewers whose investment in the ghetto tends to override all critical faculties.

The second – that films made for a mass audience are automatically suspect when it comes to representations of lesbians and gay men – still holds true for a significant number of gay film critics. Despite a growing trend towards 'queer', 'oppositional' readings within some (mainly academic) circles, the bulk of what we refer to as 'gay film criticism' still starts from the premise that what matters most is not what the film in question contributes to the art of cinema, or what pleasures it might hold for a queer-literate audience, but the degree to which it explicitly serves the gay political cause. Faced with a lesbian or gay character in a mainstream film, the question your average gay film critic feels most inclined to address is not 'does this character have an important and/or entertaining part to play in the shaping of the plot?', but 'is this character setting a good example?'.

Historically, there has always been some justification for this approach. The mainstream film industry has a poor track record when it comes to representing sexual diversity. A remarkable book for its time, Russo's *The Celluloid Closet* traced the history of lesbian and gay characters in Hollywood, pointing up the various ways in which queers were portrayed as being somehow alien to the American dream. In the revised edition published in 1987, the author added an afterword, amending his original conclusion that 'there have never been lesbians or gay men in Hollywood films. Only homosexuals',[4] and stressing that 'gay visibility has never really been an issue in the movies. Gays have always been visible. It's *how* they have been visible that has remained offensive for almost a century'.[5]

In these queer times, the limits to this kind of criticism are surely obvious. Given his overwhelming sense of 'responsibility' towards the gay cause, I doubt very much whether Robin Wood would be keen to find himself quoted in this context, but his remark about ideology having a repressive as well as an expressive function has some bearing here. Although Woods uses 'ideology' to mean the dominant values of white, Western heterosexual society, his warning could equally be applied to the field of gay film criticism: when confronted with gay ideology, it is always necessary to ask not only what it *expresses* but what it *represses*. The fact that Vito Russo found so few homosexual characters deserving of the identity 'lesbian' or 'gay' says a lot about the nature of the films he was describing, but it also says something about his personal understanding of what it means to be a gay man, and what he personally took to be 'offensive'.

In the late 1990s, there are still plenty of things to take offence at. Despite the Oscar-winning success of a film like *Philadelphia*, the Hollywood power brokers don't seem especially keen to make lesbians and gay men part of the wider picture. What has changed, I hope, is how we view those lesbian and gay characters who do make it onto the screen. If the legacy of queer has taught us anything at all, it is surely that there are many ways of expressing a gay identity, that one man's negative image might be another man's limp-wristed, poodle-worshipping, wise-cracking, knife-wielding special creation.

CRUISING: THE MOVIE

The role of stereotypes is to make visible the invisible, so that there is no danger of it creeping up on us unawares.

—*Richard Dyer*[6]

Gay people will die because of this film.

—Leaflet distributed during gay protest against *Cruising*

Raymond Murray cites *Cruising* as 'the most notorious film from the late 70s, early 80s assault of Hollywood-inflamed homophobia' before suggesting that 'having lost its power to offend, the film is now part of queer film history and a testament to how a frightened Hollywood treated a disenfranchized minority'.[7]

Shot during the summer of 1979 in New York's Greenwich Village, and released the following year, William Friedkin's leather-queen serial-killer thriller was distinguished by the fact that it was the first film to face disruption by gay activists, pre-dating the *Basic Instinct* furore by some thirteen years. Before *Cruising*, activists tended to wait and see a finished film before staging their protests. In this instance, they intervened at the production stage, confident that the 'homophobic' nature of the source material (a 1970 novel by *New York Times* editor Gerald Walker), coupled with Friedkin's reputation as the director of the much-maligned *Boys in the Band* (1970) more than justified their actions.

Cheered on by gay *Village Voice* columnist Arthur Bell, who implored his readers to 'give Friedkin and his production crew a terrible time'[8] activists did everything within their power to disrupt filming, blowing whistles to disturb the sound takes and shining mirrors onto the sets, breaking up the lighting scheme. What effect their interventions had on the finished film is open to speculation, though Friedkin's decision to open his film with a disclaimer pointing out that *Cruising* was 'not intended as an indictment of the homosexual world' was clearly prompted by the controversy.

Cruising stars Al Pacino as Steve Burns, a New York City cop assigned to track down a psychotic killer with a taste for Pacino look-alikes in leather. Apart form their physical resemblance to Pacino and passion for sadomasochism, the murder victims are united by the fact that their bodies all show evidence of anal intercourse – all with traces of semen, all devoid of any actual sperm.

When we first meet Burns, he is living what we assume to be a happy heterosexual existence. The film is as much an exploration of his repressed desires as it is an exploration of 'the gay underworld'. Having kissed a temporary farewell to his girlfriend Nancy (Karen Allen), Burns moves into a Greenwich Village apartment, assumes a new, 'gay', identity as 'John Forbes' and begins scouring the local leather bars for the killer. He is soon accepted as regular on the circuit and develops what appears to be a genuine friendship with his neighbour Ted Bailey, a gay playwright whose possessive lover Gregory doesn't take too kindly to Burns' interest.

Meanwhile, Burns and Nancy seem to grow ever further apart, so much so that his occasional visits to her bed are seen as a substitute for his newly-awakened homosexual desires. When he turns down a proposition from another man outside a club, the man responds by drawing attention to his erection: 'That bulge in your pants ain't a knife'. Burns' growing 'sympathy' with gay men is also shown in other ways. When, in one of the film's most extraordinary scenes, a large black man wearing only a hat and jockstrap bursts into a police interrogation room and threatens to beat a confession out of a potential suspect, Burns freaks out. He later tells his boss, 'I didn't come on this job to shitcan some guy because he's gay'.

Eventually, the real killer is identified as Stuart Richards, a drama student who took a class with one of the murder victims. His motive is that he has a hang-up about his sexuality, complicated by a desire to win the approval of his dead father. Luring Richards into a rendezvous at the local part, Burns taunts him into pulling a knife, stabs him and takes him into police custody. Matching his fingerprints with those on a quarter found in a peep show booth where one of the victims was discovered, the police urge Richards to confess to all the murders. He refuses.

Several days later, the police are called to the site of another violent gay murder. One of the officers at the scene is a 'shakedown cop' with a reputation for harassing gay men. The victim is Ted Bailey, Burns' friend and neighbour. Meanwhile, Burns has returned to Nancy, promising to tell her everything. While he is in the bathroom shaving, she discovers his leather jacket and cap and decides to try them on. The film ends with Nancy checking herself out in the living room mirror, while Burns gazes at his own reflection in the bathroom.

As Nat Segaloff points out in his book on 'The Stormy Life and Films of William Friedkin', *Hurricane Billy*, 'in synopsis form, *Cruising* appears as a far more unified narrative than on film, where it contains such a surfeit of nuance, digression and detail that, far from arriving at conclusions, viewers are encouraged to become stunned by the complexity of the issues'.[9] Unfortunately, gay activists didn't see it that way at all. For them, the issue was very simple – so simple, in fact, that it could be summed up in the phrase that went onto their pamphlets: 'Gay People Will Die Because Of This Film'. And before anyone could say, 'No they won't, silly', a minister's son emerged from a car outside the Ramrod Bar, one of the sites where *Cruising* was filmed, and shot down two gay men. There was nothing to suggest that the gunman had even heard of *Cruising*, let alone that it was the film and not his religious conditioning, which had prompted his actions. But no matter. The way Vito Russo recounts the incident in *The Celluloid Closet* you could be forgiven for thinking that was all the evidence required to prove that *Cruising* was a danger to the gay community, and that the activists had been right all along: 'gay people did die because of this film'.[10]

I'm not interested in speculating as to why someone proclaiming a progressive agenda and a keen interest in the politics of representation should assume such a direct, causal relationship between what is depicted on screen and what happens in the social world. To my mind, this places Russo in the company of someone like Michael Medved, who only wants to see films fit for all the family, or Andrea Dworkin, who insists on seeing every sexually explicit image as an attack on women. Needless to say, I don't believe that *Cruising* caused the deaths of anyone, any more than I believe that pornography causes rape. What I am interested in is how the controversy around *Cruising,* and the allegations made by those activists involved in the protests, helped shape gay critical evaluations of the film which followed.

CRUISING: THE CAMPAIGN

The fact of homosexuality does not guarantee *anything* beyond the given alignments of sexuality, gender and class within the social formation. What *can* be expected, and must be demanded, is an end to films like *Cruising*, which wilfully position homosexuality within a dense and mystifying field of associations with terror, violence, self-hatred and psychological disorder.

—*Simon Watney* [11]

Cruising is not about homosexuality.

—*William Friedkin* [12]

In an essay for *Screen* titled 'Hollywood's Homosexual World', Simon Watney condemns *Cruising* as 'offensive' and 'dangerous'. His argument is impassioned, if a little muddled. Having made a point of distancing himself from those critics who draw 'distinctions between supposedly "true" and "false" representations of homo-sexuality, as if there were some ideologically "correct" way of signifying gays',[13] he nonetheless slips into a discussion of the film which revolves around precisely these concerns.

According to Watney, *Cruising* is a Bad Thing because it depicts the gay world 'as an infernal domain';[14] because it 'relies heavily on the contagion theory of homosexuality';[15] because it 'posits a banal equation between actual violence and the signs of various versions of masculinity donned for the gay scene';[16] because it goes 'to great lengths to establish the murderer's motives in relation to some repressed and implicitly violent homosexuality';[17] because 'the potent image of victimization' is presented 'as if it stems *naturally* from the very fact of homosexual desire';[18] because the film 'reinforces the view that homosexuality is *intrinsically* a problem, something which requires regulation and policing, in order to protect the non-gay world from moral "pollution"'.[19]

Leaving aside, for the moment, the question of how accurate these assessments are, it seems clear that what Watney is really concerned about here is how far, in his opinion, *Cruising* confirms negative images of gay men as victims, as sexual predators, as perpetrators of

91

violence, as corrupters of all that is straight and true. In other words, he is concerned with drawing distinctions between 'true' and 'false' representations of homosexuality, using the example of *Cruising* to illustrate what is, to his mind, false, and pointing the reader in the direction of what he takes to be true. Thus he informs us that, contrary to the 'sinister' depiction of the gay SM scene he finds so 'offensive' and 'dangerous' in *Cruising*, there is certainly no one-to-one relation between sexual role-play and the hyper-maleness of the leather gender-identity. Indeed, the leather subculture is 'both a response to the historical association of homosexuality with "effeminacy", as well as a subversion of the original connotations of the style"'.[21] He also makes the somewhat contentious claim that while 'in *Cruising* homosexuality is constructed as pure sex', in reality 'the very concept of promiscuity is clearly irrelevant to gay men, existing as it does solely and purposively in relation to the ideals of marital monogamy'.[21]

At the same time, Watney is prepared to admit that, as Friedkin has always maintained, *Cruising* is not actually a film about homosexuality. In this respect, at least, he shows some insight. Unfortunately for him, his acknowledgement of this fact does tend to call into question some of his other observations. If *Cruising* is not a film about homosexuality, then how, for example, can one claim that 'it reinforces the view that homosexuality is intrinsically a problem'?

The fact that *Cruising* is not really a film about homosexuality seems to me irrefutable. It may be set in an identifiably homosexual world, it may even involve gay characters and incorporate fairly explicit accounts of homosexual sex, but *Cruising* is no more a film 'about homosexuality' than John Carpenter's stalk-and-slash movie *Halloween* is a film 'about heterosexuality'. In *Halloween*, the killer's actions are explained by the trauma of a childhood incident, in which he discovers two heterosexuals having sex. In *Cruising*, the killer's actions are explained by his attempt to repress his own homosexuality; he is, as Watney points out, literally 'killing his own desire'.[22] Given the fact that homosexuality is, at least, to the uninitiated, far more scary a prospect than heterosexuality, this seems to me to be not only a more credible motive for murder, but also one which supports the argument for doing away with the closet. In other words, *Cruising* is not a film about homosexuality, but a film about homophobia, or what many gay activists make a point of referring to as 'heterosexual panic' ('homosexual panic' in the common parlance). It isn't homosexuality which kills, but the fear of it.

For those gay activists who campaigned against *Cruising* from the outset, one of the most offensive aspects of the film was the implication that, by the final scene, Pacino's cop has somehow taken over the killer's identity. In fact, there are a number of possible interpretations of this scene. Certainly, as Burns gazes into the mirror we are led to think that he has come face to face with his own homosexuality. But this doesn't necessarily make him the murderer. As Nat Segaloff asks, 'did Gregory, Ted Bailey's jealous, belligerent, room-mate, kill him and then leave town? Was Bailey killed by the shakedown cop who, after all, has been seen in his car, at the bars, in the park, and now at the murder scene?'.[23]

Still Watney echoes the activist's objections when he complains that *Cruising* relies heavily on the contagion theory of homosexuality. It's worth remembering that Watney is writing immediately after the film's release – shortly before AIDS, and long before the kinds of queer political strategies and critical practices with which he now likes to be associated. The idea of homosexuality somehow being 'contagious' may carry greater resonance nowadays; the experiences of the epidemic call for greater sensitivity when approaching such ideas. However, a 'contagion theory of homosexuality' isn't that far away from queer activists insisting that straight society is right to fear us, that the consolidation of a 'queer nation' would result in more and more people coming out as a result of their 'exposure' to a gay way of life.

And since *Cruising* is not actually a film about homosexuality, it seems strange to charge it with promoting the idea that homosexuality is contagious. Even if we ignore the film's many ambiguities, and accept the interpretation that Pacino simply takes on the identity of the murderer, all that is being suggested is that exposure to a gay way of life has forced him to confront his repressed homosexual desires, and that, like the killer, he is unable to deal with them. For Watney, this leads to the conclusion that 'according to *Cruising*, homosexuality may be an alternative, but it is an alternative which kills'.[24] For me, it tells a rather different story. What may or may not be implied in the final scene of *Cruising* does not constitute a warning against homosexuality, but a warning against its repression. And for that, Friedkin ought really to be applauded.

CONCLUSION: GET REAL

Claim the heroes, claim the villains, and don't mistake any of it for realness.

—*B. Ruby Rich* [25]

If William Friedkin were gay, his 'offensive', 'dangerous' film would probably have been received rather differently. Compare reviews of *Cruising* to reviews of Tom Kalin's 1992 killer-chiller *Swoon* if you don't believe me. Few gay critics complained when Kalin decided to 'put the Homo back in Homicide', as the teaser for his film read. The fact that Friedkin is heterosexual, and that his film was made from a discernibly heterosexual point of view, goes some way to explaining the intensity of feeling about *Cruising*. Arthur Bell made this clear when he wrote that Friedkin's film 'promises to be the most oppressive, ugly, bigoted look at homosexuality ever presented on the screen. The worst possible nightmare of the most uptight straight'.[26] Simon Watney makes it equally clear when he complains of 'the film's overall mystification of its environment, and the sexual activity which takes place there',[27] and cites the scene where Burns enquires about handkerchief codes as an example of how Pacino's straight cop 'is cast as the innocent abroad'.[28]

Yet as Richard Dyer acknowledges in an article addressing 'some of the problems in the representation of gay people as typical', 'the development of gay subcultures meant that many homosexual people did participate in a lifestyle, a set of tastes, a language and so on that meant their lives were, in more ways than the sexual, different from that of most heterosexual people'.[29] Given this quantifiable difference, it seems inevitable that any film made from the point of view of a heterosexual man, and depicting the lifestyle, tastes and language of a gay subculture should contain at least an element of voyeurism. And despite Watney's hysterical claim that '*Cruising* effectively closes down any consideration of the continual struggle on the part of lesbians and gay men to define our own social relations and sexual pleasures',[30] the plain truth is, at the end of the day, it's only a movie.

If *Cruising* were released today, it seems doubtful that it would be damned in quite the same way that it was in 1980. The campaign against *Basic Instinct* may remind us that the days of hysterical, censorious gay activism are by no means over. Still, a number of distinguished lesbian critics have since gone on record as saying that they found Sharon Stone's portrayal of ice-pick wielding, bisexual temptress Catherine Trammell little short of empowering. As Amy Taubin 'confessed' in the *Village Voice*, 'I make no case for *Basic Instinct* as a great or even a good film. I simply got a kick out of it . . . Catherine is a bad girl who gets away with it. That's quite an anomaly in a Hollywood movie'.[31] Similarly, I make no case for *Cruising* as a great film. I simply think that its reputation as one of the most homophobic films ever to come out of Hollywood is undeserved. And yes, I do get a kick out of it.

The question now is whether viewing for kicks is ever enough. One of the arguments made against so-called queer readings is that, far from constituting a legitimate critical strategy, they are merely a convenient, fashionable way of suspending moral judgement, or dodging the responsibilities of *realpolitik*. Whatever school of thought you ascribe to, the process of watching and writing about a movie bears little relation to the dirty business of politics as it is practiced. Painful though it may be to accept, one's opinion of a film is not going to change the world. If it's *realpolitik* you're after, chain yourself to the gates of Downing Street, abseil into the House of Lords, join a lobbying group, anything – just don't become a film critic.

Besides which, there is a strong case for arguing that the kind of 'responsible' gay film criticism demonstrated by Russo, Wood, Watney *et al* is no less an exercise in avoidance. In the warm-up to his attack on *Cruising*, Watney remarks that 'to identify a stereotype is to signal one's rejection of a particular image, usually of oneself . . . It therefore involves both recognition *and* refusal'.[32] What is this, if not an acknowledgement of denial, an illustration of the repressive (and defensive) nature of ideology Wood warns against?

In his afterword to *The Celluloid Closet*, published in 1987, Russo made an appeal for 'no more films about homosexuality', on the grounds that 'the few times gay characters have worked well in mainstream films have been when film-makers have had the courage to make no big deal out of them'.[33] A decade on, it's high time we appealed for no more writing about how secure (or not) we are in our identities, masquerading as film criticism.

Notes

1. Vito Russo, *The Celluloid Closet* (Harper & Row, 1981, 1987), p. 325.
2. Robin Wood, 'Responsibilities of a Gay Film Critic', in *Movies and Methods, Vol II*, ed. Bill Nichols (University of California Press, 1985), p. 653.

3. Wood, p. 653.

4. Russo, p. 245.

5. Russo, p. 325.

6. Richard Dyer, 'The Role of Stereotypes' in *The Matter of Images* (Routledge, 1993), p. 16.

7. Raymond Murray, *Images in the Dark: An Encyclopaedia of Gay and Lesbian Film and Video* (TLA Publications, 1994), p. 393.

8. Quoted in Nat Segloff, *Hurricane Billy* (William Morrow, 1990), p. 199.

9. Segaloff, p. 198.

10. Russo, p. 238.

11. Simon Watney, 'Hollywood's Homosexual World', in *Screen*, Vol. 23, Nos 3–4 (1982) p. 120.

12. Quoted in Russo, p. 182.

13. Watney, p. 108.

14. Watney, p. 109.

15. Watney, p. 110.

16. Watney, p. 110.

17. Watney, p. 113

18. Watney, p. 112.

19. Watney, p. 112.

20. Watney, p. 111.

21. Watney, p. 118.

22. Watney, p. 110.

23. Segaloff, p. 207.

24. Watney, p. 112.

25. B. Ruby Rich, 'New Queer Cinema', in *Sight and Sound*, September 1992 (supplement), p. 6.

26. Quoted in Segaloff, p. 119.

27. Watney, p. 109.

28. Watney, p. 112.

29. Dyer, p. 21.

30. Watney, pp. 112–113.

31. Amy Taubin, 'Ice Pick Envy', in *Village Voice*, 28 April 1992, p. 35.

32. Watney, p. 108.

33. Russo, p. 326.

Chapter Eight

GAY CULTURE:
WHO NEEDS IT?
Toby Manning

In the summer of 1994 I attended a concert at the Lincoln Centre in New York, part of the Gay Games and Cultural Festival. The concert featured 'a programme of songs by lesbian and gay composers', performed by a lesbian and gay choir and featuring lesbian singer-songwriter Holly Near. This was the first occasion on which I actively felt embarrassed to be gay.

I was embarrassed by the poor quality of both music and performance, and by the rapture with which both were greeted, as if *gayness* over-rode consideration of merit. I was embarrassed by the event's relentlessly feel-good nature, exemplified by Holly Near's anthem: 'We are a gentle, loving people . . . singing for our lives'.[1] I was embarrassed by the self-righteousness with which the event kept pushing gay emotional-response buttons, a tawdry song by AIDS activist Michael Callen being greeted with reverence and tears.[2] I was embarrassed by the assumption that campness was both the height of wit, and intrinsic to a 'gay sensibility'. And it was that idea of a shared sensibility, a uniform gay identity, which – because it presumed complicity in the horrors before me – embarrassed me most of all. Not self-loathing, not 'false consciousness': just embarrassment, pure and simple.

Shortly afterwards, as part of the Stonewall riot's twenty-fifth anniversary celebrations, I went on a banned march down New York's Fifth Avenue, a breakaway event from the Mayor's moribund First Avenue route. Looking around the illegal march I realized that there was an alternative, non-straight culture which wasn't mindlessly positive, had a sense of humour about itself, and was celebratorily diverse: almost the opposite of everything that had made the Gay Games concert so abhorrent. The participants included street drag queens, skinny East Village punk boys, anarchists, prostitutes, bearded ladies, hippy radical faeries, transsexuals, people with disabilities . . . all those who don't fit in and aren't represented by mainstream gay culture. I'll explore this alternative culture later, but until then it'll mostly appear bracketed, just as it is bracketed (or excised altogether) by the gay mainstream.

Mainstream gay culture is a monolith, with clearly defined ideologies and goals, the product of three key institutions – gay political organizations, gay media and gay business. Each of these emerged directly out of the gay liberation movement of the 1960s and 1970s, although they drew on the kind of past homosexual culture lived by Quentin Crisp in *The Naked Civil Servant* or imagined by Neil Bartlett in *Who Was That Man?,* according to how they fitted either the gay political, or the gay commercial agenda. An obvious example is drag, which (leaving aside its PC margin-alization during the 1980s) while apparently providing continuity between gay culture and the homosexual past, underwent a fundamental change post-Stonewall, from a way of life to a commercial enterprise. The gay politico-commercial stranglehold on culture is revealed through certain unchallengeable givens, all of which were proudly on display at the Gay Games concert that summer day: positive images, righteousness, Gay is Good, campness and uniformity.

The propagation of *positive images* is a political tactic intended to counter negative cultural representation of homosexuality: a politics of 'affirmation'. The advocacy of lesbians and gays as 'ordinary people' (workers, partners, consumers) who simply want the same rights as everybody else is presented as 'commonsensical', but in fact represents an acceptance of the tenets and institutions of a society that oppresses the 'deviant' (including homosexuals). Rather than challenge the thinking behind taxonomies of 'deviant' and 'normal', the gay response has been to try and prove its 'normality', so gay culture places emphasis on the 'universal'– the Gay Games as 'an *affirmation* of the human spirit' (my italics), in the words of one official photo-caption; 'I am perfectly normal with one slight difference', to quote a near-blueprint letter in *Gay News*.[3] The lack of critique of this 'normality' and of society's structures leads to such dead-ends as gay campaigns for acceptance in the military and for gay marriage, and, at the gay conservative extreme, to Andrew Sullivan's *Virtually Normal* and Bruce Bawer's *A Place At the Table*.[4] 'According equal rights to homosexuals and equal recognition to same-sex relationships . . . would not threaten the institution of the family but would actually strengthen [it]'. The Gay Liberation Front's (not always convincing) attempts to pursue a more radical agenda[5] had collapsed by 1972, and thus it was largely the staid Gay Activists Alliance (US) and Campaign for Homosexual Equality (UK) that set the liberal, bourgeois, reformist tone for gay politics – and consequently culture.[6]

In order for these 'positive images' of gayness to be easily understood by the 'straight' world, all 'difficult' aspects of homosexuality are glossed over, and those whose lives place them slap in the middle of these difficulties are maginalized accordingly. Taken at random these difficulties include: sadomasochism, male promiscuity, transsexuality, bisexuality, tensions between lesbians and gay men, lesbian penis fantasies, and, simply self-loathing. What is offered instead is the feel-good, the bland, and the beautiful. Nothing exemplifies this better than gay theatre company Gay Sweatshop, for whom positive images are the *raison d'être*.[7] Past play titles tell it all: *I Like Me Like This, Any Woman Can, The Dear Love of Comrades*. Here conflict exists only between the gay and the straight; characters are one-dimensional; analysis gives way to a simplistic, reformist 'message'. Gay Sweatshop does not – as it claims – open up discussion: it closes it down.

The latest gay positive image – part of the ongoing 'gay gentrification of sexual identity'[8] – is that of the pink pound/dollar-rich consumer. This is relentlessly pushed by the new breed of gay lifestyle magazines aimed at mainstream advertisers – *Attitude* in Britain, following on the heels of *Out, Genre* and *10 Percent* in the US and finding its extreme in *Victory* – and by the marketing departments of gay consultancies like Ellie Jay Group ('Loyal, discerning, trend-setting . . . affluent' goes the blurb in its 1995 brochure). The claim is often made that this display of economic advantage (however limited its application) will bring about recognition from business and therefore *rights* from a business-worshipping political class – a curiously naive and misconceived notion.

Gay culture also patrols the representation of homosexuals in the culture at large, the gay media declaring whether artworks (homosexual- or straight-produced) are 'positive' or not. Queer writer Denis Cooper 'commits literary terrorism' according to the *Flamingo Anthology of Gay Literature* because his work doesn't 'instruct, bear witness, or affirm the right [of homosexuals] to exist'.[9] Thus is one outstanding writer damned for failing to accentuate the positive. Jean Genet is dismissed as political 'poison' by Mark Lilly in his study *Gay Men's Literature in the Twentieth Century*,[10] even as the writer's lyrical talents are extolled. Meanwhile the smugly second-rate writers such as Michael Carson (*Sucking Sherbet Lemons*), Andrew Holleran (*Dancer from the Dance*), Barbara Wilson (*Murder in the Collective*) and Jean Stewart (the *Isis* sci-fi chronicles) are feted by the gay media, simply because they offer an acceptably 'positive' image of homosexuality.

The American organization GLAAD (Gay and Lesbian Alliance

Against Defamation) has dedicated itself to eliminating the negative in American film and media, targeting *Basic Instinct* (1992) for its 'negative' portrayal of lesbianism, and harassing the scriptwriter and director of AIDS drama *Philidelphia* (1993) to 'get it right'. The gay community were far from happy with the end result, but quite how much blander it might have been had GLAAD had its way doesn't bear close consideration (although a glance at the Ikea guppy commercial might offer a clue). Queer film-maker Bruce LaBruce puts the cynical view succinctly: 'Hollywood films are not public service announcements, sweetie. As the man said, if you want to send a message, call Western Union. GLAAD and their ilk want to normalize and homogenize homos, to render us as bland and boring and inoffensive as everyone else'.[11]

Another given of gay culture is *righteousness*. Self-righteousness is perhaps an inevitable by-product of liberation movements, but gay righteousness is particularly offensive in its ability to be simultaneously apologetic and self-aggrandizing. Apologetic because it doesn't challenge the *structures* of society, it simply says 'straights are being horrid to us' (repeatedly and at great length in the gay media).[12] Self-aggrandizing because the mantra of oppression drowns out all else in its repetition, inducing an indignation out of proportion to the issue. As Erland Outland pointed out in San Francisco's *SF Times* (to a storm of abuse): 'homophobia is not the biggest problem in the world'. Nor does simply being 'visibly' homosexual automatically confer radicalism and/or worth. *Time Out* columnist Paul Burston aptly described a recent 'lesbian visibility'[13] exercise focused on a bus ride around London as 'witless exhibitionism', rather than being (as its proponents claimed) 'revolutionary'.[14]

So endemic is this righteousness that it is easily induced in a gay audience by pressing certain key emotional response buttons. These are: the trauma of 'coming out'; the Holocaust; AIDS (sometimes emotionally linked to the Holocaust); gaybashing; the need for legal equality; visibility; and increasingly the right to pleasure (amongst consumption-glutted disco bunnies who have no interest in anything they conceive as 'political'). Some of these issues are valid, but their constant, unquestioning invocation makes for dull, lazy speeches at Gay Pride festivals (of the 'I am a one-legged lesbian from Lithuania' variety); unanalytical, unobjective news reporting (see the gay media's outraged response to the suggestion that HIV might not be sole cause of AIDS; the respect given AIDS closet cases Freddie Mercury and Rock Hudson); sentimental songs that operate a kind of community thought-bypass (like those of Holly Near or Michael Callen at the Gay Games); and bland films (*Philadelphia, Parting Glances, Longtime Companion* all busily pushing the AIDS button). But these emotional response buttons are carefully chosen to keep the issues as mainstream as possible. Little righteous anger is heard on behalf of transsexuals or SM dykes. Anything that doesn't fit the righteous reformist agenda is kept out of sight, ignored in the gay press and by gay political organizations – after all, if it's not wholesome and easily understood, heterosexuals (read 'powerful, conservative figures') might be scared off.

An even wider-ranging gay cultural given is Gay is Good, the self-prescribed Prozac of the gay media and consequently the gay community; the relentless celebration of all businesses, activities, products and individuals designated gay, regardless of worth, merit or talent. Originating as part of the same politics of affirmation that produce positive images, Gay is Good soon transmuted into the idea of supporting gay organizations and individuals as community resources and figureheads. Ironically Gay is Good doesn't work particularly successfully in respect of the obvious 'community initiative' arena – the voluntary sector. Rival gay organizations bickered throughout the 1970s, and the advent of AIDS in the 1980s brought the antagonisms to new intensity. The internal and external squabbles of AIDS organizations are well documented by the gay press, as indeed they should be. But why this inconsistency in the application of Gay is Good?

The fact is that whatever the original conception, Gay is Good now functions in an almost exclusively economic way, operating as a support system for the ever-growing gay business sector, rated 'sound' because of its 'gayness', regardless of employment practice (or pricing policy). Gay businesses are given huge amounts of coverage by the gay press (which they either own or support through advertising): gay entrepreneurs are profiled, their businesses and products hyped and reviewed, their opinions quoted in news reports and features. The annual Pride festival is a key example of a gay holy of holies, an event which has moved from 'community initiative' to full-blown commercial enterprise, and has little political meaning or impact. Gay bathhouses and sex clubs are also often seen as 'community initiatives',[15] but make enormous profits out of a fixed, easily-targeted demographic. Gay culture, like all capitalistic cultures, involves promiscuous interaction with commerce, and the commercialization of its promiscuous interactions.

Gay is Good also underlies the notion of anthologizing already available texts or films under 'lesbian and gay' banners. Again, gayness replaces merit as consideration, but the real motivation appears to be economic. By tagging films simply 'lesbian and gay', the lesbian and gay film festivals have long ensured economic support from a mindlessly loyal audience for what is often substandard product.[16] Gay anthologies, such as Michael Wilcox's collections of (often embarrassingly inept) *Gay Plays* or David Leavitt and Mark Mitchell's (better but still meaningless) collections of *Gay Short Stories* and *International Gay Writing*, also do a brisk trade from the gay marketing demographic.

Gay is Good provides a solid base of support for artists and public figures designated gay, i.e. those the media declares fit the gay cultural agenda,[17] or who represent the interests of gay business. Pop music provides a number of obvious examples. Gay men troop out loyally to buy anything by Jimmy Somerville, Boy George, or Erasure, however dire, while lesbians follow suit with the second-rate sub-Springsteen rock of out lesbian Melissa Etheridge. But not all gay culture declares itself as such. For instance, the Pet Shop Boys long avoided the topic of their sexuality, but nevertheless were loyally supported by the gay community and media.[18] Hardly the sort of role models the 'coming out' gay culture should be supporting, you'd have thought? However, with the band's music and style being overtly tailored (by a gay manager, Tom Watkins) to appeal to a gay audience at the same time as a younger, female audience, the financial basis of Gay is Good again becomes apparent. The younger generation of 'boy bands' Take That, Boyzone and East 17 (who disavow suggestions of gayness much more strongly), drew in huge crowds to gay clubs as unknowns, increased the circulation of gay press once better known, and keep gay business pockets lined once they really strike pay dirt.[19] When all this is at stake, it's hardly surprising that designated gayness doesn't need to rest on declaration.

The lesbian obsession with k.d. lang has certain similarities – a singer deliberately ambiguous about her sexuality but who offers covert 'lesbian' messages – but also significant differences. Lesbians are so starved of 'role models' in popular culture that much tends to be forgiven those who apparently fit the bill but deliberately avoid discussing their sexuality – Jodie Foster being the most obvious example. Hardly revolutionary though, the covert, unacknowledged lesbian signal, unless anyone wants to argue that fashion magazines, which these days specialize in pseudo-lesbian images, are at the forefront of revolutionary sexual politics.

The insistence on Gay is Good, and the restrictive, although inconsistent application of that term, means that the scope of gay culture is incredibly narrow. How many articles about k.d. lang, Ian McKellen or Neil Tennant is it possible to read? Isn't gay culture in danger of boring itself to death?

That's where *camp* comes in. By designating those female singers, soap stars and actresses considered 'camp' as gay culture, the culture's scope is extended. However, this appropriation of second-league actresses from *Murphy Brown* and *Coronation Street*, or even first-rate comediennes like French and Saunders (who pink-pound-sensitively give the nod to their gay following) rests on the highly arguable assumption that there is something intrinsically gay about camp. This is largely derived from the foppish sensibility of the man who has become, rightly or wrongly, the godfather of gay culture – Oscar Wilde. But before Wilde the fop was a figure who, while often seen as 'unmanly', was very much heterosexual: 'Effeminacy was despised, but was not a special characteristic of the sodomite'.[20] Equally, it is rarely suggested that the campness associated with men impersonating women such as Judy Garland or Shirley Bassey is found not in the *impersonation* but in the *stars themselves*, and their participation in a long tradition of theatrical camp. The claim for camp as a gay sensibility can often seem like an attempt to appropriate the talent and sparkle of others to enliven a culture dulled by the blandishments of gay politics and gay business. And, of course, it keeps gay culture as close as possible to the mainstream.

The adoption of camp by homosexuals themselves is often viewed as 'challenging', but it's arguable that camp even at its most sophisticated – as in Wilde's *The Importance of Being Earnest* – is the politest of weapons. After all, its appeal to gay culture is always said to be connected to its manipulation of 'surface' (which presumably explains gay fascination with the twin airbrushes that are Pierre et Gilles), what Richard Dyer calls the gay 'strategy for survival'.[21] And in its often tawdry gay form – the oo-er, exclamatory gush of gay journalists, the fiasco of Channel 4's *Camp Christmas*, the affected witlessness of waiters in gay restaurants – it presents not a challenge but the reassurance that fags are just as limp and pussified as homophobes had always suspected.

Underlying this appropriation of camp, the strategies of positive images and Gay is Good, and the self-righteousness of gay culture is the assumption of *uniformity*: of a common identity and sensibility gained through a common experience of oppression (the nurture argument) or even one that is innate (the nature/'gay gene' argument). This 'sensibility' in its 1990s form could be said to encompass dance music, female comediennes, muscular bodies, designer clothes, Calvin Klein underwear, cappuccino, bottled beers and Ikea furniture. Needless-to-say there is nothing *intrinsically* homosexual about any of these things: they are simply what gay business offers (feeding off what has succeeded before, and what is reassuringly mainstream); what mainstream business cannily markets to the pink pound via the gay media and what that media then disseminates as 'official' gay culture. The consumption of the appropriate gay items comes to constitute gay 'identity', and so gayness, in its commodified, standardized form, simply becomes a marketing demographic. As British fanzine editor Mark Connorton commented: 'Gay liberation isn't about becoming a market segment'.[22] Connorton is part of a minority amongst homosexuals, most scene newcomers quickly perceiving that to be accepted as gay they have to consume in the appropriately gay way. One experience of a punk queerboy is typical: 'It's assumed that all gay people look a certain way, and if you don't you start out at a severe disadvantage'.[23]

The mindless uniformity of gay culture, as well as serving its commercial interests, also effectively serves its political imperatives, by obliterating difference and diversity even as it apparently embraces it. It is ironic that it is the fact of gay publications being 'general interest' and appealing to a 'broad demographic' that is offered as reason for not addressing (or if you prefer 'censoring') anything that actually reflects that diversity. And so gay culture must be kept bland, middle-brow and mainstream. As Michelle Crone, special events director of the Gay Games Cultural Festival said 'Our culture isn't counter . . . we're leading the mainstream in terms of creativity'.[24] Anything challenging (gender fuck, radical faeries), high-brow (Foucault, Freud) or avant-garde (queercore, queerzines) must be glossed over, attacked, or ignored.

Through its political and financial imperatives – positive images, righteousness, Gay is Good, camp, and uniformity – gay offers a culture of official mediocrity. But amongst what has been proscribed there are works, ideas and individuals which examined more closely can be seen as constituting an alternative to the monolithic under-achievement of gay culture. The radical philosopher Michel Foucault's ideas provide a useful approach to this alternative culture.

Foucault views gay liberation and, by extension, gay culture as a 'reverse discourse'[25] to the socially constructed discourse of 'homosexuality', a nineteenth-century medical categorization of a 'perversion'. Prior to the medicalization of sexuality there were only sexual 'acts', some sanctioned, some forbidden. As a result of being named, 'homosexuality began to speak in its own behalf, to demand that its legitimacy or naturality be acknowledged, often in the same vocabulary, using the same categories by which it was medically disqualified'.[26] Foucault suggests the only way to avoid reverse discourse is to reject altogether the tenets and vocabulary of the oppressive society, and to pursue the 'transgressive pleasures' of 'bodies and desires'[27] rather than societally constructed 'sexualities'. Foucault finds perfect expression of this in the life of the nineteenth-century French hermaphrodite Herculine Barbin.[28] However, as Judith Butler has pointed out, such 'transgression' doesn't avoid discourse:

'[its] pleasures are always already embedded in the pervasive but inarticulate law, and indeed, generated by the very law they are said to defy'.[29] Foucault contradicts his own assertion of the constructed nature of 'sexuality' by invoking the possibility of a return to some primal, a-societized, 'innocent' state. However, Butler's attempt to out-Foucault Foucault with a more rigorous strategy – the dissolution of identity itself – is, if anything, more impractical still, not to mention considerably less appealing. As Jeffrey Weeks says, '"Sexuality" may be an historical invention, but we are ensnared in its circle of meaning. We cannot escape it by act of will'.[30]

What we can do, however, is immerse ourselves in the very contradiction of Foucault's 'transgressive pleasures' because this offers both the basis for a dynamic, challenging cultural strategy, and a means of understanding the connections between apparently disparate figures, who together can be seen to constitute just such a transgressive culture. In contrast to gay culture, a transgressive culture operates outside the mainstream's rules, jettisons its rationales, and rejects its bourgeois morality, as part of a broader, oppositional movement of outsiders.

Jean Genet is a key figure here, one whose relationship with gay culture has never been comfortable and whose work rejects the notion of a gay identity. He associated himself with an underworld of outsiders, where homosexual acts are just one expression of a wider transgressive culture. Genet's influence is to be found throughout gay culture, but perhaps most significantly within gay porn: its isolated male-only environments; its (often uniformed) 'straight' participants, indulging in brutal, wordless sex; its stereotypical masculinity of overdeveloped musculature and over-sized members. Inevitably porn removes most of the most radical aspects of Genet (the way cissies and brutes can be combined in the same person, the way the beautiful is found in the ugly or obscene, the perception of a work of art in a crime), but even so, porn is something which gay culture locks into the bathroom cabinet, a hidden and undiscussed (though central) part of that culture. Genet's claim that 'I have decided to be what crime has made of me' has been interpreted by Alan Sinfield as a 'reverse discourse' to the societal discourse that labelled him criminal and deviant. Thus Genet's stance is linked to gay culture's reclamation of 'oppressive' symbols like the pink triangle.[31] While, as I have noted, it is impossible altogether to avoid discourse and Genet certainly *enjoyed* the status of 'outlaw', he also asserted that the way he lived was not motivated by 'bitterness, or anger, or any similar sentiment' but because he 'was *hot* for crime'.[32] This is not a 'reclamation', but a *rejection* of the very tenets and standards by which bourgeois society judged and labelled him – and by extension, everyone else. Genet turns morality on its head, celebrating criminality, cruelty, betrayal and humiliation. Many argue that this is simply a mystification/glorification of 'self-oppression', but the very notion of self-oppression becomes meaningless once the value system of the dominant society is rejected. 'Repudiating the virtues of your world, criminals . . . organize a forbidden universe',[33] a universe of outsiders, challenging the hegemony of the dominant order.

But it would be wrong to see Genet as the sole progenitor of a transgressive culture, which is simply the product of specific social conditions, such as industrialization, capitalism and the medicalization of sexuality. A fair amount of the work that appears to be Genet-influenced – for instance queer fanzines – has arrived independently at a similar position. Genet's countryman of a century before, the visionary poet Arthur Rimbaud's life and work contain the same interface of rebellion, deviance (class, sexual and racial) violence and poeticism. The archetypal outsider, Rimbaud rejected bourgeois morality, craving a 'derangement of all the senses',[34] the quest for which scandalized first the stuffy Catholic conformity of his village, and then, at fifteen-years-old, effete literary Paris, via his tempestuous, violent affair with the older poet Paul Verlaine, and their experiments with drugs and alcohol. Maurice Rollinat called him 'the genius of perversity',[35] and, appropriately enough, at the age of nineteen Rimbaud gave up poetry in disgust and spent the rest of his short life running guns in Abyssinia, dying of syphilis at the age of thirty-seven.

William Burroughs is another transgressive figure. His 1959 novel *The Naked Lunch* was described by the *Daily Mail* as 'like Genet turned into a Marx Brothers script'. Burroughs never quite fitted in anywhere, remaining an outsider figure to both straight and gay mainstreams. Burroughs' work creates an amoral universe (simply a heightened version of our own) permeated with random, seemingly unmotivated violence by criminals and law-makers alike and a gender-bending, shape-shifting sexuality (boys being fucked by girls with strap-on steam-powered dildos), which challenges the 'natural' order of society. There are many other writers who could be regarded as transgressive: look at George Bataille's murderous sexual fantasies; Jean Cocteau's polymorphously perverse anti-family in *Les Enfant Terribles*; the Marquis de Sade's deviant, lyrical ramblings; Hubert Selby's tough-lyrical, violent-camp clash of class, racial and sexual mores in *Last Exit to Brooklyn* and *The Room*. More recently there is Denis Cooper, who shows the influence of Genet, Burroughs and de Sade in his tortured, twisted fantasies of exploited, abused teenagers, predatory homosexuals and murder. 'I'm not in the official group of "new writers", Cooper said in a recent interview, 'I'm still marginal. I'm happy there'.[36]

It is arguable that although Tennessee Williams is often name-checked as a gay figure, his relationship to mainstream gay culture is far from straightforward. John M. Clum is not the only gay writer to decry 'homophobic discourse in Tennessee Williams'.[37] Certainly Williams' depiction of sad, self-hating homosexuals who have no commonality with each other and desire only well-adjusted, masculine men, runs contrary to the gay political agenda. But his depiction of homosexual and female desire is powerful, challenging (to conventions around masculinity and femininity) and often disturbing, his dissection of the patriarchal family often highly acute, and his 'homophobic discourse' inspires an electrically lyrical prose.

Foremost amongst transgressive film-makers is Rainer Werner Fassbinder, an artist gay culture has long been wary of, *Gay News* (February 1976) decrying the 'atmosphere of exploitation and seediness' of *Fox and his Friends*. Fassbinder's violent, sexual films blurred the binaries of 'straight' and 'gay' (he was bisexual himself), challenging easy assumptions, not just about sexuality, but about race (*Fear Eats The Soul*), and class (*Fox and His Friends*), and all these strains come together in his adaptation of Genet's novel, *Querelle* (1982). Some of Derek Jarman's earlier work, like *Jubilee* (1977) could be seen as transgressive in its take on class and sexuality (if often impenetrably pretentious), though he quickly became the token 'bad boy' of the gay coffee table set, and his films became accordingly simplistic (e.g. the OutRage! scene in *Edward II*).

Transgressive culture is not restricted to writing and film-making. There are transgressive photographers (Robert Mapplethorpe, Della Grace) and painters (Francis Bacon) who have shaken assumptions around race and sexuality, and there is a transgressive musical tradition, which arguably would include the Velvet Underground, with their fascination for de Sade (*Venus in Furs*), Genet (*Sister Ray)* and all forms of outsider lowlife – drug-addicts, transvestites and prostitutes; Bowie in his glam bisexual days (*Queen Bitch, John, I'm Only Dancing*); the sluttish macho-camp thrash of the New York Dolls; Robert Mapplethorpe alumnus Patti Smith's early gender- and genre-defying musical rants; Wayne/Jayne County's cross-gender terrorism; West Coast 1980s hardcoresters Hüsker Dü, a band hugely influential on queercore.

Gay Culture

Although some of these artists did interconnect, and certainly influenced each other, they are mostly isolated figures, ploughing their own individualistic furrows. But in the 1990s closer links began to be forged between those who found themselves outside both mainstream and gay society and culture. This has been, problematically, referred to as the 'queer movement', and it emerged from a punk subculture of bands, fanzine-writers and, soon enough, film-makers, which consciously rejected both mainstream and gay culture, the latter often in unequivocal, even irrational terms: 'You just don't understand, do you. *You* are the enemy, not Jesse Helms', spat *Bimbox*, a seminal Toronto zine. Subjective, unaligned and unofficial, not for profit, free of adverts (though this is now changing), queerzines disseminated the ideas of disenchanted, often working-class youth, forging links, networks, alliances, and – inevitably – enmities in the process.

Punk is integral to this subculture, what Dick Hebdige calls its 'blankness . . . the refusal to speak or be positioned'[38] ('I belong to the blank generation' – Richard Hell),[39] connecting to Genet's refusal to acknowledge the values and taxonomies of the dominant society. Queerzines spawned 'queercore' bands like Fifth Column, God Is My Co-Pilot, Sister George, L7 and Tribe 8, and a vibrant body of films. JD's co-founder Bruce LaBruce went from scribbling Genet-esque short stories to the witty, sexy and scabrous *No Skin Off My Ass* (1991) and *Super 8½* (1994), while former collaborator G.B. Jones has also produced films like *The Yo-Yo Gang*. Gregg Araki is also very much a product of this zine scene, although his refreshing insistence that he wished to depict characters 'without regard to which set of genitalia they prefer'[40] hasn't always been matched by quality. However, what Richard Dyer calls the 'liberating moral indifference'[41] of *The Living End* makes it a thoroughly transgressive film, one which sees no need to apologize, explain, or 'bear witness'.

113

Other films often grouped together under the banner 'new queer cinema' are not necessarily products of the queerzine movement, but have much in common with it: Todd Haynes' *Poison* (1991), an inspired and overtly Genet-influenced study of different forms of deviance; Tom Kalin's murderer-chic *Swoon* (1992); and Cyril Collard's *Savage Nights*. Described as 'the spiritual child of both Genet and Pasolini' in *France-Soir* (1989), *Savage Nights* for all its tedious reliance of stock male/active/controlled and female/passive/ emotional/hysterical characterization, is challenging in the way it takes bisexuality for granted, though it is this that causes gay critic Simon Watney to lambast the film in *Sight and Sound*, as it 'cannot provide [Collard] with an identity which can in any way help him to articulate his social and political predicament'.[42] On the contrary, Collard's 'predicament' is a *medical* one, and one which adherence to an 'identity' cannot ever hope to solve.

Transgressive cultural strategies can be – and have been – dismissed as individualistic and no more than gestural, doomed to remain on the margins, unable to effect real change. However, gay politics does not even *aim* for change, its assimilationist strategies seeking merely to reform society's laws. The collapse of Queer Nation is often taken as an example of the failure of queer/ transgression as a whole, though the organization in fact had no connection to the queerzine ethos, simply appropriating the term 'queer' for what was essentially just a more militant take on the usual gay reformist agenda. The extent of the organization's separation from *real* queer culture is illustrated by their sending a death-threat to Denis Cooper, a hero to queer zinesters. But it was this movement that came to represent queer in the popular imagination, the result being, as Bruce LaBruce has pointed out, that 'the Queer Nation sensibility and aesthetic merged with what [zinesters] were doing and watered it down'.[43] Unlike the queer zinesters' wholesale *rejection* of society, the new militancy was easily assimilable into gay culture. For all the arguments between lobbyists like the Stonewall Group and self-styled queer activists like OutRage!, not a great deal of conceptual ground actually separates the two, as Stonewall director Angela Mason constantly reiterates. Meanwhile, many of the visible signifiers of queer (nipple rings, tattoos and punk styles) were taken on by gays as fashion accessories, and thus stripped of their original meaning. Hardly surprising that 'queer' has come to suggest a pierced-nippled, brain-dead, club-crazy bimbo wiggling his hips to house music.[44] A new term is badly needed for the kind of genuinely radical transgressive culture that I have described in this chapter.

But whatever name is put to it, the fact remains that there *are* other means of expressing non-straight sexualities than participating in the uniform, self-righteous, camp mediocrity that is Gay Culture. There's life out there – beyond this political-, media-, business-constructed monolith. The question is whether gays and lesbians, saturated with a culture which offers unchallenging, superficial, cosy familiarity and worth-by-association can be bothered making the effort necessary to achieve such a life.

Notes

1. 'Singing For Our Lives' by Holly Near, from *Singer in the Storm*, Chameleon Records, 1990. Near eventually changed the words to 'We are a gentle, angry people'. As author James Robert Baker put it: 'even the world's most sanctimonious PC candy-ass finally saw the folly of coming on like Bambi Nation' (quoted in US fanzine *Fuh Cole* No. 4).
2. Michael Callen, 'Love Don't Need A Reason': 'Love don't need a reason / love don't always rhyme / and love is all we have for now / what we don't have is time'.
3. *Gay News*, January 1976.
4. Bruce Bawer, 'Notes on Stonewall: Is the Gay Rights Movement Living in the Past?'. *Christopher Street*, No. 216.
5. The GLF were notable for their attempts to blur notions of 'gender' with their 'radical drag', and attempts to create links with other radicalized 'minorities' such

as feminists (unsuccessfully) and (even less successfully) blacks. Black Panther Huey Newton's (shortlived) declaration of support for Gay Liberation now seems an unthinkable scenario.

6. Jeffrey Weeks, *Sex, Politics and Society* (Longman, 1981, 1989).

7. See Philip Osment's introduction to *Gay Sweatshop – Four Plays and a Company* (Methuen, 1989).

8. Matias Viegener, 'The Only Haircut that Makes Sense Anymore', in *Queer Looks*, ed. Martha Gever, John Greyson and Pratibha Parmar (Routledge, 1993), p. 128.

9. *In Another Part Of The Forest: Flamingo Anthology Of Gay Literature*, ed. Albert Manguel and Craig Stephenson (Flamingo Original, 1994), p. 15.

10. Mark Lilly, *Gay Men's Literature in the Twentieth Century* (MacMillan, 1995).

11. Bruce LaBruce, 'Obsession', *Sight and Sound*, March 1995.

12. Terry Sanderson's 'Media Watch' column in *Gay Times* is the most obvious – and relentless – example of this, a space for the meticulous recording of every (often laughable) slight against the gay 'community'.

13. 'The theme of Pride 1995', Paul Burston in *Time Out*, 29 February 1995.

14. Carellin Brooks, 'Lesbian Avengers Manifesto' in *Time Out*, No. 1296, June 1995: 'Maybe if he'd seen the faces in Marks and Spencer when we made our impromptu visit to the lingerie department, he wouldn't have been quite so dismissive of our revolutionary potential'.

15. For example, Randy Shilts' account of the early days of the AIDS epidemic *And The Band Played On* describes the debate around the mooted closure of the bathhouses being conducted almost exclusively in terms of 'community initiatives'.

16. However, giving credit where it is due, the Festival has improved massively in recent years, with the 1995 season in particular showing the strong influence of queer ideas.

17. For instance: Ian McKellen, Elton John, Simon Callow, Derek Jarman.

18. The 'coming out' of Neil Tennant in *Attitude*, August 1994, retrospectively justified this support for many gays.

19. 'Money is a predominant factor in my life. It's vital that I'm rich'. – Tom Watkins, manager of East 17, quoted in *Attitude*, June 1995.

20. Alan Sinfield, *The Wilde Century* (Cassell, 1994), p. 37.

21. Richard Dyer, *Now You See It* (Routledge, 1990), p. 284.

22. Interviewed by this author in *Gay Times*, February 995. Interestingly the title of the article became 'Sex, Not Market Segment', effectively trivializing Connorton's point and rendering the article sufficiently 'sexy' for *Gay Times* readers.

23. Story reported from *Maximumrocknroll*, in the seminal San Francisco queerzine *Homocore,* No. 5.

24. Quoted by Alisa Solomon in 'Queer Culture – a Celebration – and a Critique', *Village Voice*, 21 June 1994.

25. Michel Foucault, *The History of Sexuality, Vol. 1* (Vintage, 1990), p. 101.

26. Foucault, p. 101.

27. Foucault, p. 157.

28. Analysis of Foucault's *Herculine Barbin, Being the Recently Discovered Memoirs of a Nineteenth Century Hermaphrodite*, in Judith Butler, *Gender Trouble* (Routledge, 1990), pp. 94–106.

29. Butler, p. 98.

30. Jeffrey Weeks, *Against Nature* (Rivers Oram, 1991), p. 166.

31. Sinfield, pp. 196 –7.

32. Jean Genet, *The Thief's Journal* (Penguin, 1987), p. 8.

33. Genet, p. 5.

34. Arthur Rimbaud, letter to George Izambard, quoted in *Illuminations*, trans. Louise Varese (New Directions, 1957), p. 27.

35. Enid Starkie, *Arthur Rimbaud* (Faber, 1973).

36. Denis Cooper, interviewed by Elizabeth Young in the *Guardian*, 1 October 1994.

37. Ronald R. Butters, John M. Clum and Michael Moon (eds), *Displacing Homophobia: Gay Male Perspectives in Literature and Culture* (Duke University Press, 1989), p. 152.

38. Dick Hebdige, *Subculture: The Meaning of Style* (Routledge, 1979), p. 28.

39. Richard Hell, *Blank Generation*, Sire Records, 1977.

40. Gregg Araki, from press release accompanying *The Long Weekend* (1989).

41. Richard Dyer, interviewed by this author for 'Jaded Days' article on queer culture in *Gay Times*, March 1994.

42. Simon Watney, 'The French Connection' in *Sight and Sound*, June 1992.

43. Bruce LaBruce, interviewed for US queerzines feature 'From a Queer Perspective' by this author, *Gay Times*, December 1994.

44. In an article in the left-wing magazine *Red Pepper*, Stephen Maddison describes queer as being about 'selling your transgressive chic down the gravy train of respectability'.

Chapter Nine

MOVE OVER DARLING:
BEYOND THE DADDY DYKE
Suzanne Patterson and Anne-Marie Le Blé

I know you've seen the type: no tits, no cock, oozing with a kind of vulnerable 'masculinity' and sheathed in a 50s style black leather motorcycle jacket or, to put it slightly differently, it's James Dean with a clit.
—*Sue Golding*[1]

Yes, we've seen the type. She is your average pool-playing, DMs booted dyke who thinks that more than two inches of hair on your head marks you as a traitor to the cause and a candidate for hetero hell. And we're not talking 'drag king' here (which *may* be a more playful take on masculinity and gender). We are talking about the 'essential' butch dyke, the one who would like to take up all ideological space within dyke culture.

It is rather strange that Sue Golding should present us with her dominant archetype of dykedom as an aspirational figure for lesbian culture in the 1980s and 1990s. But then we want to argue that this 'James Dean with a clit' is merely another example of how 'queer theory' and recent academic debates around cross-dressing and parody, butch and femme, have sometimes, contrary to their own 'transgressive' publicity, merely served to rationalize drearily predictable notions about what constitutes an 'authentic' lesbian image. In short, we want to reveal this 'debate' as a narcissistic monologue.

In what functions as an introductory disclaimer, Golding asserts that there is no 'truth as such' in her article, it is presented as some kind of postmodern fiction. To elucidate the historical roots of this erotic stereotype, Golding invokes the mutilated spectre of a mid nineteenth-century hermaphrodite who was dissected after dying in prison. Instead of analysing the story in terms of an abuse of power by the legal, medical and patriarchal systems, she uses this as a vehicle to express martyrdom and the final 'victory of the present day lesbian hermaphrodite'.

> Ignobly, her body is killed off while she feverishly reaches out to maintain her *manhood*, in all its sordid and mutilated glory. Remarkably enough, she does not die in vain.[2] (our emphasis)

Death, glory and male heroism are all present within this rhetoric. The modern counterpart of the woman (this time not a *biological* hermaphrodite) emerges as a 'virile girl', 'the butch baby, full of attitude, but not of scorn, lots of street smarts and a bit of muscle'. She is seen as sexually subversive, an embodiment of *'virile* promise' (our emphasis); she is a 'slightly more dangerous creature'. And where does this danger, this subversion lie? Golding certainly suggests by her language that it is by appropriating 'masculine' signifiers that the lesbian hermaphrodite can achieve this. Whilst acknowledging this lesbian as a biological female, she also has the 'erotic masculine'. This modern lesbian hermaphrodite has all the iconographical allure of James Dean.

> She is James Dean all over again, James Dean with the arrogant hair, James Dean with his tight black denim, James Dean with the bitter brat look, James Dean with the morbid leather looks, James Dean against the whole boring suburban middle-class, James Dean deader than a door nail, wedge into anti-hero.[3]

Again, we have the (anti?) hero and maleness combined. The subversion of this icon is not only sexual, it is now political (e.g. 'against the whole boring suburban middle-class'), which is a persuasive way of making the James Dean dyke look attractive. In fact, if this does not convince the (presumably dyke) reader, Golding asserts that her J.D. dyke is a 'defiler of the prudish world, be that world filled with lesbians or straights. In the eyes of the prudish world, the female hermaphrodite can only be pornographic filth'. The evocation of a 'prudish world' makes it difficult for the reader to disagree and therefore be implicated in repression.

But what if the reader is not part of this world of 'ignorance and hate', but merely unimpressed by the rhetoric of boyish rebellion? For example, considering the case of Dr Moreton Stille who in his 1855 *Treatise* asserted that female sexual subversives must be *ipso facto* hermaphrodite (i.e. have male physical characteristics), Golding rightly notes with disdain their argument: 'What could possibly account for that kind of aggressiveness except to say that somewhere lurking in the body of that rebel was the presence – in whole or in part – of a man'.[4] It is ironic that Golding should undermine her own argument by using the same rhetoric as the doctors she criticizes, i.e. invoking the presence 'in whole or in part' of a man to signify the female rebel. This rebel, according to Golding, is not biologically male, but a 1980s erotic fiction. However, she rejects the idea that her James Dean dyke is using an ironic acknowledgement of the ways in which society enforces gender-specific clothing depending on the kind of sexual organ between one's legs. She is not interested in parody or drag. In which case, what are we left with? A strangely seamless hybrid of 1950s iconography who lays claim to some kind of authenticity. Golding even goes as far as to declare her a 'signature for lesbianism itself'.[5]

Surely there are lesbians who do not wish to have the James Dean dyke usurp their own signature. For in all the talk of 'virility', 'manhood' and 'pre-pubescent tomboyism', we feel excluded. For with every mention of the 'virile girl' there is always the question of who is this supposedly pathetic creature, the 'non-virile girl'? If the

James Dean dyke is the signature for sexuality, rebellion, even 'creative, raw energy', then are the other dykes prudish or insipid, conformist, unoriginal? Sue Golding's article by its limits and omissions seems to imply this.

Judith Butler, in her essay 'Imitations and Gender Insubordination', discusses the elements of drag. She avows that 'there is no original or primary gender that drag imitates, but gender is a kind of imitation for which there is no original'.[6] In this anti-essentialist argument she talks about the 'naturalistic effects of heterosexual genders', claiming that these imitate 'a phantasmic ideal of heterosexual identity'. So, therefore, there is no realism in the heterosexual image, just a fantasy ideal. To perpetuate this idealized image, Butler argues, heterosexuality is condemned to 'an endless repetiton of itself'. In its attempts to fix this fantasy, heterosexuality is bound to fail and has to reinstate its own fantasy image, the 'theatrically-produced effects' which posture as normality and reality. (In this segment Butler posits male/female heterosexual behaviour as part of a masquerade.) By this negation of the 'truth' or autonomy of heterosexuality, Butler refutes charges that queens / butches / femmes are imitations of some heterosexual 'reality'. The idea is that if there was no primary reality, there can be no derogatory reference to the secondary, the copy. This is a fair point to make, but as Butler continues, the prejudices of her thinking become evident. She asserts that:

> The parodic or imitative effect of gay identites works neither to copy nor to emulate heterosexuality, but rather to expose heterosexuality as an incessant and *panicked* imitation of its own naturalized idealization.[7]

It is difficult to believe that gay parody exists purely for the purpose of exposing the charade of heterosexuality (although it may do this as a sort of by-product). Butler states that:

> Heterosexuality always in the act of elaborating itself is evidence that it is perpetually at risk, that it 'knows' its own possibility of becoming undone: Hence, its compulsion to repeat, which is at once a foreclosure of that which threatens its coherence.[8]

Sad to say, there are butch dykes to whom this quotation might apply. There is an obsessively acted-out butchness in some dykes who fear a failure of their 'masculinity' and who have to assert themselves as the 'real' thing against other types of lesbians (e.g. femme, feminine, 'lipstick', etc.) whom they consider to be frauds. This compulsory repetition is central to Butler's argument about the precarious position of the institution of heterosexuality. She then goes on to ask the question: 'what will constitute a subversive or de-instituting repetition?'. The answer to this, at least partially, is the role-playing of lesbian butch/femme. Carefully pointing out that sexuality may exceed definitive narrativization, Butler goes on to assert that 'there will be passive and butchy femmes, femmy and aggressive butches . . .'.

Butler present the butch/femme couple as some sort of paradigm (however unfixed and subject to mutability) of subversion and de-instituting repetition. Examining role playing, Butler writes:

> A butch can present herself as capable, forceful, and all-providing and a stone butch may well seek to constitute her lover as the exclusive site of erotic attention and pleasure. And yet, this 'providing' butch who seems *at first* to replicate a certain husband-like role, can find herself caught in a logic of inversion whereby that 'providingness' turns to a self-sacrifice, which implicates her in the most ancient trap of feminine self-abnegation.[9]

Butler continues to describe this 'inversion' which can bring pleasure to the butch and the way a femme can also 'invert into a butch', either being 'caught up in the spectre of that inversion', or delighting in it. Although we agree with Butler that the 'husband-like role' assumed by the butch may not be directly structured by heterosexual roles, we would take issue with the very terminology she uses to describe these relationships.

Is there any real necessity to allocate to lesbians definitions like 'butch' and 'femme' at all? Regardless of how malleable these categories may be (femmy butches and butchy femmes, etc.) these definitive titles, however convincing within the framework of Butler's article, are not credible when examined. For example, what *is* a butchy femme or a femmy butch and how do they differ? Is a butch still essentially a butch, however femmy she might be, and vice versa? These categories indicate a need for the 'sign of lesbian to be left permanently unclear'.[10] As Butler says in her introduction, 'To Theorise As a Lesbian': 'Identity categories tend to be instruments of oppressive structures or as the rallying points for a liberatory connotation of that very oppression'.[11] It seems that within the article, she has implicated herself in the reassertion of identity categories (butch and femme), perhaps under the noble intention of political subversion, but at the expense of upholding the very 'regulatory regimes' she seeks to deconstruct. The point is not to condemn butch and femme role-playing as far as sex is concerned, but to give it any kind of systematic subversive political value seems utterly ridiculous.

In Sue-Ellen Case's essay, 'Toward a Butch/Femme Aesthetic', arguments similar to Butler's are employed, with Case rejecting the supposed realism of heterosexuality in favour of the subversive qualities of camp irony. Case, however, also falls into the trap of designating the butch/femme couple as the way out of oppressive heterosexual roles. 'The lesbian roles of butch and femme, as a dynamic duo, offer precisely the strong subject position the movement requires'.[12] Here the butch/femme couple is seen as playfully subverting fixed gender roles:

They are the coupled ones who do not impale themselves on the poles

of sexual difference or metaphysical values, but constantly reduce the
sign system through flirtation and inconstancy into the light fondle of
artifice.[13]

This all sounds rather too simply resolved. Another example of this
is Case's analysis of Joan Riviere's 'masquerade' in the light of
butch and femme role-playing.

Unlike Riviere's patient, these women play on the phallic economy
rather than to it. Both women alter this masquerading subject's
function by positioning it between women and thus foregrounding the
myths of penis envy and castration in the Freudian economy. In bar
culture these roles were often acknowledged as such. The bars were
abuzz with the discussion of who was or who was not a butch or
femme and how good they were at the role. In other words, these
penis-related posturings were always acknowledged as roles, not
biological birth rights, nor any other essentialist poses.[14]

Case presents the butch/femme lesbians as using camp to subvert a
'Freudian mythology'. She seems to say that in bar culture there was
always an awareness of the way that butch and femme functioned to
highlight the heterosexual myth. But it is questionable whether
lesbians in the 1950s were genuinely aware of the butch/femme
roles as a politically subversive act which served to expose the
constraint of the 'masquerade'. The position of the 1950s dyke was
more complex, and Case is applying her theories to the 1950s with
1980s hindsight. Like Butler, Case is keen to point out the anti-
essentialist standpoint of the butch/femme dykes and yet what does
she replace this rejection of realism, this possibility of play or choice
with?

Her answer is to be found in the 'penis-related posturings' of the
butch and femme. Whilst ostensibly free of heterosexual mythology,
it seems that they are condemned 'to play out' its gestures, albeit

with awareness that it is just a game. There is a paucity of imagination which constantly posits the butch and femme couple as a unit, as the only possible saviour of lesbian sexuality, when, theoretically at least, essentialist ideas are being challenged and there is the prospect of more diversity. The insistence on irony as a tool to counteract the negative effects of hetero-realism seems to be flawed. As Case says: 'The female body, the male gaze and the structures of realism are only sex-toys for the butch/femme couple'.[15]

But can butch/femme couples live their whole lives immersed in camp irony, and could they in the 1950s bar culture which Case cites? The problem with Case is that she makes it sound too easy. She states in her final paragraph:

> In recuperating the space of seduction, the butch/femme couple can through their own agency move through a field of symbols like tiptoeing through two lips (as Irigaray would have us believe) playfully inhabiting the camp space of irony and wit.[16]

Case seems caught up in her own wishful thinking about this dreamland of butch and femme role-play.

Carole-Anne Tyler adresses the significance of camp in current lesbian and gay theories in her essay 'Boys Will Be Girls: The Politics of Gay Drag'. She talks about the re-evaluation of camp, which was formerly relegated to a lowly status within gay culture and has now been hailed as a 'postmodern strategy for the subversion of phallocentric identities and desires'.[17] Camp has been inserted into different rhetorical paradigms, yet as Tyler says, camp should be approached symptomatically rather than automatically branded radical or conservative; camp is 'not a unitary phenomenon'.[18] In an examination of misogyny within gay culture, Tyler notes that the attitude of many gay men to the phenomenon of drag is 'I don't usually make it with drag queens – none of the guys do' (quote from the film *Outrageous*).

Tyler recognizes that camp or 'feminine' attributes still have a long way to go within gay male culture (this observation could be extended to include lesbian culture). She notes that 'it does not follow that because gay men are unafraid of being seen as gay they are unafraid of being seen as feminine (where femininity signifies castration in a patriarchal fantasmic).[19] This quotation could be applied to a butch lesbian who might fear being seen as 'feminine'. There are butch lesbians who take such issue with the 'feminine' that they are only attracted to other butches. This attitude is strikingly similar to that of the gay male macho who only associates with others of the same type, deploring camp or femininity. It is possible that many lesbians are currently gravitating towards the gay male macho image, as illustrated by certain tendencies under the queer banner. As Linda Semple says:

> Dykes had to take the models of gay male sexual practice, apply them to lesbians' sexual practice, and say 'what if?'. There was an intellectual and theoretical need to align with gay men around the politics of representation and sexuality which had been hijacked by radical lesbian feminists.[20]

It is not surprising that some lesbians, tired of the soft focus image associated with lesbian sex, have wanted to challenge these clichés by borrowing from gay male sexuality. An example of this is the attempt to emulate what is seen as strictly the domain of gay male sex, such as cruising on Hampstead Heath. 'When lesbians bemoaned the lack of cottaging for lesbians, men suggested they go on the Heath too'.[21] Although the whole ritual of cruising can be liberating for some women, it is hard to see how this would create equality with gay men. Under the title 'Learning From the Boys' Cherry Smyth puts forward the opinion that 'the language of gay male sex and the public space for its enactment are more developed and specific and have no doubt increased the articulateness of lesbian sexual expression'.[22] Although lesbian sexuality has for a long time suffered from censorship, one cannot generalize and assume that cruising and having sex in public places will necessarily liberate and enlighten lesbians.

This theme of 'teaching' lesbians or women is common in various texts. Returning to Tyler, she looks at Leo Bersani and his misogynist view of women in his essay 'Is the Rectum Grave?'. Bersani is also upholding the revered gay macho ideal, saying that gay camp serves to deconstruct the negativity of feminine images: 'A certain type of homosexual camp speaks the truth of that femininity as mindless, asexual and hysterically bitchy'. And Bersani has the arrogance to suggest that his parody of femininity can have the power to enlighten and instruct women on their position: '. . . helping to deconstruct that image for women them-selves'.[23] Yet the gay macho image is not attributed the same deconstructing powers to enlighten men, but is accepted in a 'naturalized' way: 'Gay men are the better women, represented as better equipped to undo identity', Tyler says of Bersani.[24] If gay camp is seen as revealing the construction of feminine identity and its flaws, then butch-acting lesbians should have the same parodic effect of deconstruction – which is by no means the case. It seems difficult to argue that most butch dykes adopt a pose out of an irresistible desire to undermine stereotypes of masculinity, whereas perhaps drag-queens act out of a sense of fun and temporary identity change. Cherry Smyth, in her discussion of Della Grace's photograph 'Lesbian Cock' addresses the issue of envy and the adoption of male inspired attitudes.

In this delicious parody of phallic power laced with an envy few feminists feel able to admit, these women are strong enough to show they're women. Their pose encapsulates their desire for the upfront cruising style, the eroticization of the ass, casual sex, cottaging, penetration and the economic power and social privilege of the gay male.[25]

127

This statement brings up many questions, such as why is this photograph described as parody? It seems that the term 'parody' is a convenient blurring technique, used to disguise the obsession some dykes have with gay male culture. The issue of envy is also skimmed over with the assumption that there is truly something to be jealous of (eroticization of the ass, cottaging, etc.). The impulse here is to emulate and compete with gay men rather than send them up with parodic humour. It is true, however, that the 'drag king' phenomenon is not necessarily always just a case of jealousy, and it would be simplistic to suggest this. Much depends on the attitudes of the women involved, and also of their interpreters, critics, writers, and cultural mediators. There are many different approaches to parody – for example the playful analysis of male stereotypes as explored by performance artist Diane Torr, who offers the women attending her workshops the opportunity to role-play and dissect some of the more ludicrous aspects of male behaviour, from seedy businessman to indie boy.

But Smyth defends the adoption of a *gay male* image, assuming that this is in itself parody, and implying that the women who take this stance are actually undermining male power. The attitude is 'Hey daddy, almost fooled ya! See here, your look isn't so very macho, so transgressive, for we can take it further'.[26] Therefore dressing up like a leather queen, wearing a false moustache and sucking or packing a dildo will undermine machismo and reveal its flaws? And how does the gay man feel about such emulation?

Smyth assumes that 'the gay man in return admires the butch's assumed masculinity, fetishistically packed in leather'. So how far has this parody been successful in terms of a critique of macho gay behaviour? If we are to believe Smyth, the boys have even given it their seal of approval. But Smyth herself acknowledges that gay men do not fetishize the cunt and breasts or 'learn from the girls', and that, if there is male camp or drag, it refers to heterosexual women, not lesbian codes. As Smyth says:

> If dykes assume daddy/boy codes, they are mirroring a powerful
> aesthetic of masculinity, when gay men reflect back mummy/girl
> codes, which have no fetishized sexual purchase yet, even for dykes,
> you have a parody of, or homage to, heterosexual femininity.[27]

Smyth is here revealing the power imbalance between lesbians and
gay men and her own inclination towards gay male culture,
dismissing the eroticization of a strong femininity within lesbian
culture. It seems that 'queer' dykes have understandably reacted
against 1970s style feminist censorship, but in doing so have taken
gay male culture as a model for rebellion. According to Della Grace,
'lesbians even have gay male sex'.[28] This attitude is seen as
liberating. Smyth states that 'Queer culture and politics herald a
lesbian and gay sexuality which is sexual, sexy, and subversive'.[29]
But as Elizabeth Wilson points out:

> Transgression is never *per se* radical, but historically has been linked
> to extreme right as well as left-wing and apolitical stances.[30]

So much for the theory. In fact, examining popular attitudes on this
subject, we can see that 'queer theory', rather than being 'transgressive' or 'subversive' is in many ways simply an elaboration of
'common sense' assumptions held by many lesbians. It may be an
extension of an ideology which has become so ingrained in dyke
culture as to appear 'natural', (e.g. the generally accepted notion that
butch is best, the comparative ease with which the 'naturalized'
butch integrates into the lesbian scene. Of course, things are
changing even within the timescale of writing this essay, but this
atmosphere has certainly been prevalent in recent dyke history.

Much has been made recently of the importance of the *visibility* of
lesbianism, which is somehow seen in itself as a political act. It may
be that there are parts of queer and dyke theory which ignore wider

political issues in favour of a radicalism which centres purely on sexuality, sexual practices and display. This *literal* visibility appears to be all-important to many lesbians, with its covert assumption that to be visually recognizable on the street is necessarily a political end in itself. But if we look at the area of, for example racism, the existence of black civil rights struggles has actually counted for much more than the mere fact that black people are obviously *seen* to be non-white.

Here we have Teresa de Lauretis elucidating the dilemma of the invisible femme. She gives the example of Mary, the 'feminine' partner of Stephen Gordon, hero(ine) of Radcliffe Hall's *The Well of Loneliness*:

> Even today, in most representational contexts, her (homo) sexuality being what cannot be seen, she should enter the frame of vision either *as* or *with* a lesbian in male body drag.[31]

It is presumed that a lesbian can only be defined by the presence of a butch, or by being a butch herself. This reductive definition raises the question of whether there can be other ways of being visible – such as by using speech, writing, or action. Just because a woman may not look butch (what is derisively termed as 'passing'), does this automatically make her mute and incapable of any subversive or political action? Quite often these lesbians are criticized for their lack of an identifiable image on the streets, while their more visually explicit sisters are praised for their stance. It is assumed that the latter are somehow 'carrying the can' for the others, as in a letter to the *Pink Paper*:

> Those butch dykes were the ones who carved the tunnels, so that you'd have room to breath.[32]

Another letter printed in the same issue attempts to explain exactly why butch women adopt a particular style, and in the process reveals quite a lot of prejudice about the 'femme' look:

> Dykes don't exactly want to 'look like men' but want to look like
> people who are strong, competent, self-possessed, unvictimized, etc.
> Because men are traditionally supposed to have these characteristics
> and women are not, it can be hard to express these qualities in their
> dress without appearing to 'dress like a man' . . . 'why can't gay
> women look like women? And behave accordingly?' You sound just
> like my mother. Should we: wear make-up, have long hair, sit with our
> legs together, display submissive body language, be quiet, fit in?

This letter speaks for itself, with its assumption that the only form of
autonomous expression and strength should necessarily be linked
with male imagery, and its mindless equation of the accoutrements
of 'femininity' (long hair, etc.) with submission and silence. Here is
another letter, again with an 'anti-femme' slant:

> We don't want men . . . and we don't want to be approached by them,
> which is likely to happen if we're 'passing' dressed in a dress, high
> heels and long hair. If we are attacked we've got more chance of
> getting away and at least we know we didn't *ask for trouble*.[33] (our
> emphasis)

Whilst a publicly 'out' stance may indeed be admirable in its risk-
taking attitude, it is a choice which should not have to necessitate the
put-downs associated with those who do not belong to this category.
Instead of berating a society which creates problems for us, much
effort is made to blame other women, in a similar way that women
have been blamed in 'straight' discourses. The butch often emerges
as a hero, the 'passing' lesbian as a traitor, and even worse if she
dresses up, she is the archetypal slut who asked for it. None of this
seems to be addressing the real problem – which is about anti-
women attitudes in our society generally. Whether a woman is being
jeered at on the streets for being too butch, plain, or too overtly

'pretty' or 'tarty', it is like two sides of the same coin – there is a prescriptive misogyny about how we should look:

> Being a femme presents its own difficulties. A warped misogyny is present in this liberated land: Big sister provides her own diktats of political rectitude and rules on sexual mores with an oppressiveness that discourages individualism.[34]

The notion of literal visibility sometimes can be taken to the position of assuming that you *are* what you wear. It seems that there are some who still believe in butchness as an *essential* (non-parodic) state, to whom what we wear is crucial, and which determines how we should be judged. Taken to its conclusion, this could mean that SM lesbians who use Nazi paraphernalia are actually supporting the ideology suggested by their clothing, which is a ludicrous proposition that SM dykes would be the first to deny. This is merely an example of how visual signifiers are not fixed. Therefore, is it not possible to say that women who want to play with signifiers of 'femininity' should be entitled to do so without being accused of aping heterosexuality or opting for easy solutions by conforming to a femininity which is dictated by patriarchy? For there are distinctions between a 'femininity' which is imposed on women and one which is acknowledged and controlled by women with the power to subvert heterosexual norms.

One way in which lesbians have become more visible lately is via the concept of 'lesbian chic'. This is a media operation which has claimed and popularized lesbianism as a topic for consumption in both fictional narratives (soap scripts, advertisements, etc.) and in so-called 'real-life' (in magazine and newspaper profiles). There has been a recent preoccupation with this theme – from forays into lesbian subculture to the high profiling of stars such as k.d. lang.

This media fascination for lesbianism has opened up many of the debates that we have mentioned earlier. Judging by articles and letters in the lesbian and gay press, this phenomenon has elicited many heated opinions, and the tendency has been to polarize the debate. On the one hand there are those who applaud all the media attention, arguing that any exposure is good exposure, and on the other hand there are those who vehemently reject the hype, decrying the lack of more 'real' (i.e. less 'femme') stereotypes. Della Grace's comments in *Diva* typify this:

> What is 'lesbian chic' and who are we taking about anyway? Could this signal the emergence of the lesbian chick, i.e. a lesbian who doesn't force herself down the throats of unconsenting others, who doesn't take up too much space (read: thin) and who calls herself gay, bisexual, possible lesbian, but never dyke. Who are these lesbian chicks? The two nice girls on the cover of *Newsweek* last year?[35]

In this passage Grace seems to be saying that the 'chicks' who are described as *thin* (i.e. flimsy?) are unable to identify as 'real' dykes. They are unthreatening and passive, as if their very body shape dictated their political stance. They are seen as 'good' girls (in the pejorative sense), and they are judged by their looks much in the same way that men have previously judges women, as brainless 'bimbos' if they are too overtly 'feminine'. Grace's unfounded supposition is that these women dare not use the word dyke. Similarly in a *Time Out* article, Della Grace complained about dyke representation on TV: 'Shit, they've all got long hair. They're all *girly* [our italics] . . . I mean I've grown my beard in protest'.[36]

However, it is evident that not every dyke on TV fits this profile, and that Grace has been selective in her analysis. For example, Hufty, ex-presenter on *The Word* fitted another stereotype: no hair, baggy man's suit and big boots. Rhona Cameron and Donna Mcphaill, both comedians and TV presenters aren't exactly known for their 'girly' behaviour either. Grace can barely mask her prejudices against lesbians who choose not to look butch. The term *girly* is symptomatic of this kind of attitude.

Both polarities of the lesbian chic bad/good debate seem to be using the arguments in a simplistic way. There are those who defend the idea of 'positive' role models – attractive (passing) women such as *Brookside*'s Beth Jordache *et al.* To others (such as Grace) the idea of 'positive' role models has quite another meaning and they equate the use of pretty and long-haired (i.e. femme actresses) as negative, and complicit with mainstream culture.

In this argument, there has been some ideological confusion. The first point which is being made, that these characters are being created as an object of consumerism, is a fair assessment. However, mixed with this valid argument is a covert critique of the 'femme' image, as though having long hair is evidence of reactionary politics *per se*.[37] Again the 'femme' image is relegated to the realms of backward fantasy, and there is a call for the 'real' dyke. This insistence on 'reality' is particularly naive. Some lesbians have complained that dyke characters should even be *played* by dykes. Here is an excerpt of a reply to an earlier letter which was printed in *Capital Gay* (23 October 94):

> *Eastenders* for role models? Is she serious? Get real, lady. Straight women paid to play the part of straight-acting gay women? No dearie. The real role models should be real dykes . . . Caroline's pretty little brain might be better focused on why such parts aren't played by real dykes.

You can't get more essentialist than this – and again we have the equation of 'prettiness' with stupidity. On the question of soaps, are we really supposed to believe that, for example, Beth from *Brookside* (actress Anna Friel) should be a real murderess, or that the actor who plays her father should have been a wife batterer? Taken to its logical conclusion, this way of thinking is ridiculous, and betrays an ignorance of the concept of 'fiction'.

In fact this 'real' dyke debate existed long before the 'lesbian chic' circus began, but many women have used recent events as a focus for their long-held prejudices and beliefs. Putting aside the ethics of media manipulation, this issue has become a vehicle for the 'femme/anti-femme' debate.

Lesbians have fetishized specific elements of gay male iconography and have also developed their own cult of male heroes. The 1950s have inspired many dykes with icons like James Dean and Marlon Brando who symbolized youth, rebellion, raw sexuality and subversion. These styles also became signifiers of lesbianism, linking masculinity with female homosexuality. In the 1980s and 1990s, similar 'masculine' or 'boyish' styles and dress codes are being reworked and used by lesbians to connote themes of rebellion against the straight world and sexual potency, and also to give lesbians visibility and a sense of belonging to a specific subculture.

Gay men have moved from the traditional 'effeminate' stereotype (whereas on the whole, lesbians seem to be retaining their traditional butch look) and are now playing with a number of images without compromising their gay identity: camp, macho, leather queen, drag or straight acting. As Elizabeth Wilson points out:

> The homosexuals of the mid-70s wanted to make the statement that fags were no weeds, that manliness has no necessary connection with sexual orientation. Out of this came the 'Clone' look. In a way, the clone was a caricature of masculinity . . .[38]

Obviously, the clone represents now the acceptable face of male homosexuality. It symbolizes the white, middle-class, professional gay man and has become a derided stereotype amongst some gay men who regard it as outmoded. But it is quite revealing to see that at no point in lesbian history has an excess or caricature of femininity symbolized lesbianism. Femininity has been in most cases associated with passivity and powerlessness. The 'feminine invert' as nineteenth-century pathologists called her, has at various times been denigrated and labelled a 'lesser' lesbian by psychoanalysts and also by radical feminist lesbians. She has been accused of 'passing' and has never been given political validity. As Elizabeth Wilson argues:

> Many feminists assume that there is a 'real self' beneath the artifice of fashion and that the feminist identity is simply to allow this 'real self' to come out, but such distinction between artifice and nature can no longer be maintained.[39]

We are all aware that some images of femininity projected by the media in general can be flawed and of no value and interest for re-appropriation, but the contempt for anything to do with the 'feminine' has created a monolithic and stagnant stereotype. If there is the option of butch and femme role-playing, daddy and boy games, etc., then a re-evaluation of some aspects of 'femininity' should be considered as part of identity play. In *Shebang* magazine there was an article with the subtitle: 'From Androgynous Twinning to Butch and Femme Romancing: How Do We Express Our Femininity As Dykes? Does It Even Exist?'. Reading this title posits the feminine lesbian as a perfect oxymoron. Dykes cannot be feminine because they're dykes. This is why a re-examination of femininity can be useful, particularly if one looks at the concept of the 'masquerade'. We know that femininity is socially constructed, there is no 'real' feminine essence which is biologically determined; thus as Mary Ann Doane suggests:

> The theorization of femininity as masquerade is a way of appropriating this necessary distance or gap, in the operation of semiotic systems, of deploying it for woman, of reading femininity differently.[40]

If we look at the representation of strong female characters in fiction, the *femme fatale* of the 1940s *film noir* seems worth some attention. Mary Ann Doane describes her as:

> The figure of a certain unease, a potential epistemological trauma. For her most striking characteristic, perhaps, is the fact that she never really is what she seems to be. She harbours a threat which is not entirely legible, predictable or manageable . . . She's an ambivalent figure because she's not the subject of power but its carrier . . . in a sense, she has power despite herself.[41]

The *femme fatale* represents castration anxiety, and although she generally has to be punished or killed within the narrative, she threatens and destabilizes the male protagonist. We do not wish to instate her as a positive figure, but she disturbs by embodying a very active and dangerous sexuality. She has power over men (and undoubtedly over women). Her mixture of glamour and danger makes her an interesting and powerful character. She epitomizes a femininity which is not pathetic. Lesbians have re-appropriated James Dean, perhaps they should also re-appropriate Joan Crawford, Lauren Bacall and Barbara Stanwyck, or recently Linda Fiorentino in *The Last Seduction*, a modern *film noir.*

It is important not to ignore the problematics implied with the 'masculinization' of lesbian culture, as Tania Modleski points out:

> The post-feminist play with gender, in which differences are elided can easily lead us back to our 'pre-gendered' past where there was only the universal subject – Man.[42]

But surely within the parameters of constructed femininity there are many options which do not have to signify weakness, sexlessness and subordination. Without reclaiming the 'feminine' lesbian as a new 'signature for lesbianism itself', there must be space within the lesbian paradigm for diversity, instead of the current situation, whereby the butch, androgynous lesbian boy, daddy, drag king, etc.

occupy most of the theoretical and visual space in current urban lesbian culture. Our point is not to discredit her as simply 'male defined' or 'pretend man', nor obviously to replace her with an 'essentially feminine' lesbian, but rather to look at the possibilities of subversion and pleasure within other lesbian identities.

Notes

1. Sue Golding, 'James Dean: The Almost-Perfect Lesbian Hermaphrodite' in Tessa Boffin and Jean Fraser (eds) *Stolen Glances: Lesbians Take Photographs* (Pandora Press, 1991), p. 198.
2. Golding, p. 200.
3. Golding, p. 202.
4. Golding, p. 200.
5. Golding, p. 202.
6. Judith Butler, 'Imitation and Gender Insubordination', in Diana Fuss (ed.) *Inside/Out – Lesbian Theories, Gay Theories* (Routledge, 1991), p. 21.
7. Butler, p. 22–23.
8. Butler, p. 23.
9. Butler, p. 25.
10. Butler, p. 14.
11. Butler, pp. 13–14.
12. Sue-Ellen Case, 'Towards a butch-femme aesthetic', *Discourse* No. 11 (Fall/Winter 1988–89), p. 56.
13. Case, pp. 56–7.
14. Case, pp. 64–5.
15. Case, p. 70.
16. Case, p. 71.
17. Carole-Anne Tyler, 'Boys Will Be Girls: The Politics of Gay Drag', in Diana Fuss (ed.) *Inside/Out*, p. 32.
18. Tyler, p. 29.
19. Tyler, p. 37.
20. Linda Semple, quoted by Cherry Smyth, *Lesbians Talk Queer Notions* (Scarlet Press, 1992), pp. 26–7.
21. Semple, p. 29.
22. Smyth, p. 42.
23. Leo Bersani, quoted by Tyler, p. 38.

24. Tyler, p. 38.
25. Smyth, p. 43.
26. Smyth, p. 43.
27. Smyth, p. 44.
28. Smyth, p. 44.
29. Smyth, p. 59.
30. Elizabeth Wilson, quoted by Smyth, p. 34.
31. Teresa de Lauretis, 'Sexual Indifference and Lesbian Representation', in *Theatre Journal*, No. 40 (1988), p. 177.
32. Letter titled 'Butch Dykes Deserve Respect' (reply to an admittedly silly letter which claimed there are 'Too Many Butches'), *Pink Paper*, 23 September 1994.
33. *Capital Gay*, 23 September 1994.
34. Chloe, 'self-identified femme', quoted by Jessica Berens in 'Sisters Without Mercy', *Arena, BBC2 TV*, October 1994.
35. Della Grace, *Diva*, No. 1 (1994), p. 11.
36. Della Grace, *Time Out*, 21–28 June 1995.
37. It could be argued that Beth Jordache is a positive role model. subverting heterosexuality and delivering retribution to men, but this side of her character is obviously negated by her long hair! In fact any discussion of the merits of soap characters is extraneous to our argument.
38. Elizabeth Wilson, *Adorned in Dreams: Fashion and Modernity* (Virago Press, 1985), p. 202.
39. Elizabeth Wilson, quoted in *Stolen Glances*, p. 53.
40. Mary-Anne Doane, *Femme Fatales: Film Theory and Psychoanalysis* (Routledge, 1991), p. 37.
41. Doane, p. 1.
42. Tania Modleski, 'Lethal Bodies', in *Feminism Without Men* (Routledge, 1991), p. 163.

Chapter Ten

A CASE FOR THE CLOSET*
Bruce LaBruce and Glenn Belverio

As the show begins, Judy Garland's song 'Come Rain or Come Shine' plays over the opening credits: *Closet Talk with Glennda Orgasm and Judy LaBruce.*

Glennda Orgasm and Judy LaBruce are live on the set of their new chat show *Closet Talk*. They both sport 'XXX Gay' T-shirts by fashion designer Kitty Boots.

GLENNDA: Hi! Welcome to *Closet Talk*. I'm Glennda Orgasm . . .

JUDY: . . . and I'm Judy LaBruce.

GLENNDA: Today's theme is 'A Case for the Closet'.

JUDY: You know, I really support the closet these days, Glennda.

GLENNDA: Yeah, I do too, and there's a lot more room in the closet because so many celebrities have left the closet – Amanda Bearse from *Married With Children*, Herb Ritts . . .

JUDY: Neal Tennant from the Pet Shop Boys – that was an exercise in futility.

GLENNDA: Yeah. I feel that all these celebrities coming out of the closet has contributed to gay culture becoming very mediocre – it's taken the mystique out of homosexuality.

* Written and directed by Bruce LaBruce and Glennda Belverio for *The Glennda and Friends Show* on Manhattan Cable TV, Channel 69; originally broadcast 1995.

JUDY: Why can't homosexuality be an invisible influence on art and culture and the media? That's what I don't understand.

GLENNDA: This has become a problem, Judy. What are we going to do about this?

JUDY: Well, what I think we should do is re-cap our movements over the past few years in order to bring people *abreast (the pair jut out their Wonderbra-padded chests to drive the point home)* of our dalliances.

GLENNDA: Yes, let's go over the three X's.

JUDY: We started out gay, and then we became ex-gays because we wanted to try something new, even back in the eighties, so we decided to become Punks . . .

GLENNDA: Yeah, we joined the Punk Movement because we were attracted to the music and the style . . .

JUDY: Great eighties Punk style. When we went to Hardcore shows it wasn't a sexual identity thing, it was just an aesthetic question for me.

GLENNDA: Right. Maybe we groped a cute Nazi skinhead in the mosh pit, but that's as far as it went.

JUDY: But then when Punk became co-opted and hit the runways of Paris it was time to abandon ship. So that's when we decided to forge ahead and start the Post-Queer Movement which some of you may have seen on a previous show.

GLENNDA: That was getting back to our gay roots.

JUDY: That was fun for a while, but actually it started getting a bit unhealthy, I think.

GLENNDA: (*reminiscing with a hint of maudlin mistiness*) Those all-night orgies, the endless live poppers and dead champagne, piano bar marathons – it was beginning to have a bad effect on our health and psyches.

(Cut to clips of GLENNDA and JUDY recklessly snorting amyl nitrate on the West Side Highway and shirtless men dancing in a dark disco).

JUDY: *(in confessional mode)* I never really told you, but near the end I was getting really tired of those piano bars.

GLENNDA: You were? I was getting sick of them too, but you seemed to be having a good time so I didn't want to say anything.

JUDY: I was rolling my eyes behind your back.

GLENNDA: I knew the last straw was when we started eating in Chelsea – we contracted every strain of hepatitis known to mankind.

JUDY: I think I was up to 'Q'.

GLENNDA: *(disturbed, as if noticing a slightly yellow skin tone peeking through Judy's foundation)* Yeah . . .

JUDY: What we've decided with our new movement – our XXX Gay Movement – is, well, we were ex-ex-gays, or former ex-gays, which means we were back to being gay again, albeit the gay lifestyle of pre-eighties activism, when it was more exciting, the 'Boys in the Band' / 'I Could Go On Singing' model, but now we're rejecting it all again, and actually we're rejecting 'gay' in general. The gay community must be destroyed.

GLENNDA: Yes. It's kind of like Superpostmodernism; we start a new movement every five minutes and this is the *movement du jour*: XXX Gay.

(Cut to a clip from Bell, Book, and Candle, *a 1959 Hollywood film made by the team of George Axelrod and Richard Quine, about a glamorous beatnik witch [Kim Novak] who longs to become an ordinary human. In this scene she is in a club talking to her aunt [Elsa Lanchester], also a witch).*

KIM: Auntie, don't you ever wish that you weren't what we are?

ELSA: *(appalled)* No!!

GLENNDA: We recently went on a little field trip to the Aesthetic Realist Foundation hoping to be cured – it didn't quite go the way we hoped it would . . .

JUDY: No! We ran into a few hurdles that we didn't anticipate, but . . . let's roll the clip.

GLENNDA: Yeah, let's just show the clip – let's let the audience see what we're talking about.

(Cut to GLENNDA *and* JUDY *in their good fur coats standing in a sarcastic little espresso bar.* JUDY *sips demurely from her espresso demi-tasse as they speak).*

GLENNDA: Judy, where are we?

JUDY: I don't know, is this Soho or something?

GLENNDA: Yeah, it's the art section of New York City.

JUDY: Oh my god, We're in an espresso bar right adjacent to the Aesthetic Realist Foundation.

GLENNDA: Are you having enough espresso to float Fire Island, Judy?

JUDY: I certainly am, and I'm getting all hyped up for the mêlée to follow.

GLENNDA: We're about to go to the lecture at the Aesthetic Realists – each week they analyse a different work of art according to their philosophy of beauty and the power of opposites brought together.

JUDY: Opposites – as opposed to 'homo' things, which are two things that are the same, which is *wrong*, which is why homosexuality is *wrong*.

GLENNDA: *(nodding vigorously)* Yeah, it's not normal. Penis fits vagina.

JUDY: I'm finding it really difficult to fight the tyranny of Nature every day.

GLENNDA: I can't stomach that every day. It's a lot of work. Sometimes it's easier just to go with the flow of Nature.

JUDY: We just want to be more natural. Homosexuality is not normal. We want to relax for a while and explore our bisexual responsiveness.

(Cut to a shot of the 'Aesthetic Realist Foundation' banner flapping in the wind of rainy Greene Street. Cut to JUDY and GLENNDA with a small entourage of camera people carrying Leicas, three-D cameras, video and Super-8 cameras – the whole enchilada – as they enter the building and walk into a smallish lecture hall where an art criticism talk is already in progress).

WOMAN LECTURER: . . . Beauty is the making of opposites . . .

(A visibly agitated man wielding a metal folding chair quickly approaches the drag duo).

VISIBLY AGITATED MAN: *(nervously eyeing our camera crew)* You can't film or videotape in here.

(He is momentarily distracted by the whirring sound of the Super-8 camera, and moves past the duo in an attempt to block the filming of the scene).

VISIBLY AGITATED MAN: *(to camera crew)* Stop it!

(JUDY and GLENNDA inch their high heels further into the room).

GLENNDA: *(whispering)* I don't think they like us here, Judy.

(The small crowd applauds as the speaker finishes).

GLENNDA: Oh . . . Yay!

(The VISIBLY AGITATED MAN returns to try to shoo the queens and the camera crew out of the door).

VISIBLY AGITATED MAN: *(firmly)* Please leave.

GLENNDA: We're here for the cure.

VISIBLY AGITATED MAN: *(ignoring our request)* Out! Now! Immediately!

(He unceremoniously shoves the girls out the door as a paparazzi clicks a camera flashbulb in his face. Cut to a clip from George Cukor's The Women: *an older woman stands with Roz Russell at a department store counter behind which stands Joan Crawford, playing a salesgirl. A series of chimes is heard).*

OLDER WOMAN: Oh! What's that?

JOAN CRAWFORD: Closing time!

ROZ RUSSELL: The Bum's Rush in melody, dear.

(Cut to JUDY and GLENNDA: standing outside the building in the rain,

trying to open their umbrellas, recovering from the Edna Saint Vincent mêlée of a few minutes ago).

GLENNDA: Judy, what happened?

JUDY: Well, we just tried to go in for the cure and they weren't very cooperative.

GLENNDA: They pushed us out!

JUDY: We just wanted to sit down and watch the lecture . . .

GLENNDA: And he said 'No!

JUDY: *(imitating Helen Lawson in the dressing room scene from* Valley of the Dolls) 'OUT!!'

GLENNDA: Should we try again?

JUDY: Right now? *(They laugh at the thought of it)* I think the door's probably locked.

GLENNDA: They locked us out. This is hopeless. We're doomed to being gay for the rest of our lives.

JUDY: It's back to the poppers, I'm afraid.

GLENNDA: Yeah, and the Judy Garland records. Well, there are other cults . . .

JUDY: Yes. Maybe we should try Scientology.

GLENNDA: Yah. Let's go to Scientology.

JUDY: They have more money . . .

GLENNDA: . . . and more psychotherapists . . .

JUDY: . . . and they're more sensitive to celebrities and their plights.

GLENNDA: They're like the Betty Ford Clinic of homosexuality recovery.

JUDY: (*looking up at the Aesthetic Realist banner*) I think this is more like the low-rent cure, for socialists who don't want to be gay.

GLENNDA: I didn't want to interrupt the lecture because I think it's important to be polite.

JUDY: Oh, definitely. We didn't want to barge in like some Queer Nationalists who have no sense of social decorum.

(*Cut to another clip from the brilliant* Bell, Book, and Candle, *with the two witches, Kim Novak and Elsa Lanchester, continuing their talk):*

KIM: I wish I could just spend some time with some everyday people for a change.

ELSA: You wouldn't like it, darling. They're ordinary, and humdrum.

KIM: (*wistfully*) Yes, I suppose so, but it might be pleasant to be humdrum once in a while.

(*Cut to* JUDY *and* GLENNDA: *approaching the Aesthetic Realist Foundation again*).

GLENNDA: Judy, I think we should try again.

JUDY: We're really desperate for the cure.

GLENNDA: And we're from the press and we want to help them.

(*Note: The Aesthetic Realists frequently refer to themselves as 'Victims of the Press', often wearing buttons saying as much, owing to the shoddy treatment they claim to have received at the hands of the media, whom they have attempted to boycott*).

GLENNDA: *(buzzing the intercom buzzer beside the door)* Hello?

JUDY: *(peeking in at the receptionists)* They're ignoring us!

VOICE FROM THE INTERCOM: The gallery is closed!

GLENNDA: We're from the press and we're ending the boycott.

JUDY: We want to talk to somebody about your philosophy.

GLENNDA: Do you think we should press the buzzer again, Judy?

JUDY: Sure! I'll just lean on it for a while. (*JUDY puts her finger on the buzzer and leans on it casually for several long seconds*).

INTERCOM: Could you please stop buzzing our buzzer?!

JUDY and GLENNDA: *(together)* What!? What?

JUDY: I think she said, 'Could you please stop leaning on our buzzer? It's really bothering us'.

GLENNDA: This is just like in *Breakfast at Tiffany's* when Holly Golightly kept losing her key and she had to buzz Mr Yunioshi.

JUDY: And he'd say (*imitating Mickey Rooney's post-racist performance*) 'Missus Gorightry, I protest!'

(Cut to the clip from this most excellent 1961 Audrey Hepburn vehicle directed by Blake Edwards, based on the Truman Capote novella and, ironically, adapted for the screen by George Axelrod, who also wrote the screenplay for Bell, Book, and Candle. *Cut to a married couple approaching and JUDY and GLENNDA on the steps of the Aesthetic Realist Foundation).*

GLENNDA: Are you Aesthetic Realists?

WOMAN: *(turning to her husband nervously)* Are we?

MAN: (*nervously*) I don't know what it means.

GLENNDA AND JUDY: (*together*) This is the Aesthetic Realist Foundation.

WOMAN: Oh. Well, we think that we are, actually.

JUDY: Can we ask you a few questions about the philosophy of your organization?

WOMAN: (*giggling nervously*) I don't think we can answer that right now.

JUDY: We just want to be cured of our homosexuality.

GLENNDA: Yeah, we don't want to be gay anymore.

WOMAN: Well, why not?

MAN: (*shrugging shoulders*) That's your choice, no?

JUDY: But isn't that part of your philosophy?

MAN: (*glancing nervously through the glass entrance door as it anxious to escape his inquisitors*) I don't know what the philosophy of Aesthetic Realism is.

JUDY: We heard that you could be cured of your homosexuality because the aesthetic that they're talking about is that opposites are the aesthetic ideal . . .

GLENNDA: Yeah, man and woman together.

JUDY: Yeah, and therefore two men together or two women together . . .

MAN: (*interrupting*) That's a personal choice.

WOMAN: I think if that's how you feel, there's nothing wrong with it.

GLENNDA:(*demonstrably disappointed by their liberal attitudes*) Oh, really? Are you sure?

JUDY: That's too bad, because we really want to get cured.

GLENNDA: We want the cure

MAN: That's our choice too, if you want to.

GLENNDA: That's why we're here. We're exercising our freedom of choice – to be cured. But they won't let us in. Can you go in and tell them that we're very nice people . . .

WOMAN: I can't believe that they won't let you in.

(The man starts buzzing the buzzer).

GLENNDA: They kicked us out. It was a quasi-mêlée.

MAN: Quasi? *(He seems to roll the word around in his head for a few seconds)* Why not.

WOMAN: We'll see if we can talk them into it.

JUDY: We just want to talk to them about that issue and see if they can help us.

WOMAN: Okay.

GLENNDA: *(earnestly)* Thanks for your help.

(GLENNDA and JUDY turn towards the camera as the couple buzzes the buzzer repeatedly).

JUDY: It's nice to meet friendly members of the organization.

GLENNDA: Yeah, and we're obviously in need of help.

INTERCOM: Sorry, we can't let you in.

JUDY: Uh-oh!

GLENNDA: See, they're not letting their own members in. Something's up now.

JUDY: It must be a very exclusive organization if they won't let their own members in.

GLENNDA: It's like the 21 Club – very exclusive – or the Stork Club.

JUDY: Oh dear. *(To couple)* You can't get in either?

WOMAN: I think you're right. They're definitely anti-gay in there.

MAN: Or anti-something, anyway.

(The couple leaves).

GLENNDA: I think they just have poor manners.

JUDY: *(in a 'hey, wait a minute!' mode)* But we want them to be anti-gay.

GLENNDA: *(in a 'hey, you're right!' mode)* Yeah, we're anti-gay, too.

JUDY: *(definitively)* Yes! We're anti-gay.

GLENNDA: Let's go tell them that. *(Prances over to the buzzer and buzzes it)* Hello?

JUDY: Hello. *(Presses buzzer)* We're anti-gay!

GLENNDA: We are anti-gay, really! Don't be fooled by appearances. *(Giving up)* I don't know, Judy.

JUDY: *(sighing)* It's so hard. Even if you want to do something right they won't let you.

(Cut to an establishing shot of street signs: the corner of Bedford and Christopher Streets. GLENNDA and JUDY are in front of a nearby XXX video store. They flank a white, middle-aged ordinary man, presumably gay and not long out of the closet).

JUDY: (*to ordinary man*) We're thinking of going back in the closet.

GLENNDA: Yeah, we're trying to go back. It's all about the closet.

ORDINARY MAN: (*confused*) Are you serious?

JUDY: (*smugly*) Yep.

GLENNDA: Oh, yes, we're not being sarcastic. People think we're being sarcastic, but we're not.

JUDY: No.

ORDINARY MAN: (*gesturing towards GLENNDA'S ensemble*) But you're so beautiful, you wouldn't want to hide in there.

GLENNDA: Oh, we still want to be drag queens.

JUDY: Yeah, we'll still be drag queens.

ORDINARY MAN: Oh, okay. Well, that's too bad, all the progress that's been made and people feel that they want to go back in.

GLENNDA: *(with extreme scepticism)* What is all this 'progress' I've been hearing about? What is this catchphrase 'progress'?

JUDY: We're dubious about the achievements of the gay community. We're actually anti-gay.

ORDINARY MAN: (*visibly upset*) Oh. . . uh. . . what does that mean, exactly?

JUDY: I think that homosexuality should be an invisible influence in culture. It shouldn't be something that's ghettoized or flaunted; it should be an invisible influence on style, fashion, the media . . .

GLENNDA: (*helpfully*) Cinema.

JUDY: . . . and that is its strength. If it's confined to a specific identity or to a specific geographical location or any kind of ghettoization, it becomes watered down and leads to mediocrity.

GLENNDA: We're very concerned with the mediocrity of gay culture.

ORDINARY MAN: (*trying to keep up*) So it's sort of become a mass movement? It's not an elite thing anymore? Is that what you mean by 'mediocre'?

JUDY: Yeah, in a way. It should not be about 'Professional Gay' where your whole life and identity is centred around being gay. That should be just one aspect of a full and varied life.

GLENNDA: Also, the great homosexual, Oscar Wilde, said, 'Great art can never escape the elitism of talent and the tyranny of appearance'.

ORDINARY MAN: (*surrendering*) Heavy, that's heavy for me today.

GLENNDA: (*with the air of a hipster*) Well, we're heavy. Judy and I – we're heavy folks.

JUDY: Heavy.

GLENNDA: Thanks for being on the show!

(*The ordinary man, clearly disoriented, leaves. Cut to JUDY and GLENNDA back in the studio on the set of* Closet Talk. *They are seated with a bearded, forty-something man, who sits between them*).

GLENNDA: Welcome to the book section of *Closet Talk*, and we have the author of an XXX Gay book, *User*, by Bruce Benderson. Hi Bruce!

(*JUDY displays the book with a Vanna White-esque flair*).

BRUCE: It's very nice being on *Closet Talk* and you know, you are getting a little more masculine which makes me very, very happy.

GLENNDA: Yeah, the cure is starting to work. We took some pills.

BRUCE: I don't know if you're getting more masculine or more tacky by losing the couture look, but whatever it is, I like it.

JUDY: It's kind of 'butch' drag.

GLENNDA: Yah, butch drag.

BRUCE: Yeah, it belongs in a saloon, and should your transformation continue I'll be very interested because I only sleep with straight men. For that reason I think Aesthetic Realism is a marvellous process because it puts more straight men in the world for me to seduce. I don't like sleeping with fags at all.

(JUDY flexes her bicep muscle with a limp wrist as BRUCE speaks.)

JUDY: We're creating more men for you to sleep with with our movement.

BRUCE: *(lustfully, to JUDY)* And I do look forward to your transformation too, doll.

JUDY: *(blushing)* Oooh la la!

GLENNDA: *(as if touting a new wonder product)* With XXX Gay, it opens up your options; you can sleep with straight men, women, children, animals, vegetables, minerals, everything!

JUDY: Except lesbians.

GLENNDA: Well, that goes without saying.

BRUCE: Yeah, I hear they only sleep with each other, although occasionally they do get pregnant, but I think it's mostly an artificial insemination process.

JUDY: Turkey baster.

GLENNDA: That's going against nature.

JUDY: Yeah, that seems unnatural.

GLENNDA: I can't stomach that daily quarrel with Nature.

BRUCE: I'm sure a monthly quarrel with Nature is enough for anybody. It's called a period.

GLENNDA: You know a lot about that – you're into women, too. You're bisexual.

BRUCE: *(matter-of-factly)* Yes, I'm very interested in women and their organs, I find the vagina an extremely attractive organ, I've often had oral contact with it, and what's really exciting about it is the vagina often has contact with the penis, and penises interest me a great deal, Glennda.

JUDY: Penis *fits* vagina.

BRUCE: Yes, it does!

GLENNDA:That's the tag-line of the day.

JUDY: Let's not forget that. It's a simple rule for kids to remember.

ALL THREE TOGETHER: Penis fits vagina!

JUDY: Read our lips.

(Cut to GLENNDA and JUDY flipping through a copy of Vamps and Tramps: New Essays by Camille Paglia*).*

GLENNDA: The next book on the XXX Gay reading list is *Vamps and Tramps* by Camille Paglia.

JUDY: One of our favourites here on *Closet Talk*.

GLENNDA: I'm going to read a passage that is part of our XXX Gay philosophy: 'Homosexuality is not "normal"'. On the contrary, it is a challenge to the norm; therein rests its eternally revolutionary character. Note I do not call it a challenge to the *idea* of a norm. Queer theorists – that wizened crew of flim flamming free-loaders – have tried to take the poststructuralist tack of claiming that there is no norm, since everything is relative and contingent. This is the kind of silly bind that word-obsessed people get into when they are deaf, dumb, and blind to the outside world. Nature exists, whether academics like it or not. And in nature, procreation is the single, relentless rule. That is the norm. Our sexual bodies were designed for reproduction. Penis fits vagina: no fancy linguistic game-playing can change that biologic fact'.

JUDY: (*slightly overwhelmed*) Wow! I've often thought that but I've never had the balls to say it.

GLENNDA: She enables us to say these kinds of things.

JUDY: I'll read my favourite quote from Camille: 'Helping gays learn to function heterosexually, if they so wish, is a perfectly worthy aim'. Hello! (*spontaneously bursting into song*) Hello, Bluebird, hello! Ooops! (*catches herself*) I haven't gotten over my Judy Garland phase yet.

GLENNDA: (*chastising her*) You're slipping back into Post-Queer!

JUDY: Anyway, I do really believe that, and she goes on to say: 'If counselling can allow a gay man to respond sexually to women, it should be encouraged and applauded . . .'.

(*JUDY and GLENNDA applaud as if at a golf match*).

GLENNDA: Yay for counselling!

JUDY: (*continuing*) '. . . not strafed by gay artillery fire of reverse moralism. Heterosexual love, as Hindu symbolism dramatizes, is in synch with cosmic forces. Not everyone has the stomach for daily war with nature'.

(Cut to clip of Camille on The Dick Cavett Show *talking about the banning of* Glennda and Camille Do Downtown *by several prominent gay and lesbian film festivals. Mr Cavett ponders the name 'Glennda Orgasm' for a few seconds, then twists it around into one of his famous anagrams: 'Margo's Danngle').*

JUDY: I totally do not support the Gay Games.

GLENNDA: Me neither.

JUDY: I think they should be abolished. Really, who wants to see a bunch of mincing, wheezing homosexuals who can't even make it to the finish line?

GLENNDA: Because they've consumed so much Special K [designer club drug] and Martinis the night before.

JUDY: Exactly.

GLENNDA: And you know what it's really about – it's about gay athletes who aren't professional enough or athletic enough to compete in the legitimate Olympics.

(Cut to a clip from Jerry Lewis The Nutty Professor *in which Jerry, as the nerdy, weakling professor, strains unsuccessfully to lift a heavy barbell. The weight plunges to the floor along with his now elongated arms).*

JUDY: I can see them competing in the Special Olympics.

GLENNDA: They might as well merge the Gay Games with the Special Olympics.

JUDY: Actually, there's a new theory – you were telling me about it.

GLENNDA: Oh, yeah, that new pop psychology theory. I was reading about it.

JUDY: It's where you can tell an innate gay physiognomy. . .

GLENNDA: (*puzzled*) 'Physiognomy'. Isn't that that new boutique on Rodeo Drive?

GLENNDA: (*impatiently*) No, that's 'Hypocrisy'. But you know how sometimes when you look at homosexuals you can tell just by looking at them that they're gay? They have innate physical attributes that are specific to people who are born gay.

GLENNDA: It's like, you've slept with one of them, you've slept with them all.

JUDY: That's it, exactly.

GLENNDA: Well, isn't it kind of like Down's Syndrome?

JUDY: Yah, you could say that.

GLENNDA: (*mischievously*) Like Mongoloids.

JUDY: That's the name of our new XXX Gay fashion magazine: *Mongoloid.*

(*Cut to a shot of the obviously fake cover of a book called* The Real Stonewall. *An actual book,* The Real Anita Hill, *has been clumsily doctored by obliterating all but the last two letters of 'Anita Hill' and replacing it with 'Stonewa').*

GLENNDA: This new book – it hasn't hit the bookstores yet but we've just received a reviewer's copy – it's by David Brock, author of the shocking *The Real Anita Hill*, which was an exposé of the Clarence

Thomas/Anita Hill trials – has a new book out called *The Real Stonewall: The Untold Story.*

JUDY: I've made some notes about the book so I'll just run it down quickly. The argument, basically, is that Stonewall wasn't really a gay bar. This is what has been exposed . . .

GLENNDA: It was actually an Irish sports bar.

JUDY: . . . and there actually were no drag queens there, these alleged drag queens were actually just ugly women who were hanging out at the bar, and there was some kind of dispute over an unpaid gambling debt, apparently, over some rugby game. It was just basically your typical barroom brawl. And gay leaders, always the opportunists, seized upon this barroom brawl – just because it was, you know, in the vicinity of Greenwich Village – and they trumped it up into this propaganda vehicle to start the Gay Movement. The whole Gay Movement was just a front, in the beginning, for laundering tax-free charitable funds in order to acquire real estate on Fire Island. That's his argument in a nutshell.

GLENNDA: How do gays and lesbians feel now? You've been lied to for the past twenty-five years. I bet you feel like a buncha suckers!

(Cut to vintage 1950s clips of an educational film on how electro-convulsive therapy is useful in curing homosexuality. A homosexual is strapped down to a laboratory table while a doctor places an electrified metal tongue depressor in the fag's mouth. Several young sailor types hold the patient down while he is being administered the therapy. Voice-over: 'The belief that homosexual men and women could be cured exposed them to the very latest in medical technology. These are some of the methods doctors employed to cure homosexuality: electro-convulsive therapy, or shock').

GLENNDA: *(yelling at Judy, who is nodding off)* Judy! Do you think it's okay to watch a clip from our favourite movie, *The Boys in the Band*, as a sort of Post-Queer last hurrah?

JUDY: It's funny you should mention that. I just happened to bring along a video copy of *Boys in the Band* so we could do some Aversion Therapy.

GLENNDA: (*doing his Judy Holliday routine*) Aversion Therapy. Is that like shiatsu?

JUDY (*trying to cover GLENNDA'S mouth à la Dianne Weist in* Bullets Over Broadway) No, no. No. Don't speak! What it is is electric shock therapy. In order to cure homosexuals of their affliction, they're shown scenes of the homosexual lifestyle while simultaneously being administered an electrical shock.

GLENNDA: Wow! That sounds pretty radical.

JUDY: Yeah, but you can actually do it at home with a common household fork. (*JUDY hands a fork to GLENNDA*) A table fork. Here's one for you. . .

GLENNDA: Wow! DIY.

JUDY: . . . and a common electrical socket. (*JUDY gestures towards a socket situated on the wall between their chairs*). So now we'll watch a scene from the first two-thirds of *Boys in the Band* – because the last third already constitutes aversion therapy in and of itself . . .

GLENNDA: Yeah, the 'telephone scene'.

JUDY: Yeah, it's pretty brutal. So we'll watch a scene and then we'll do the therapy.

GLENNDA: (*excited, in 'baby discovers' mode*) Okay!

(Cut to Boys *scene in which four fags are doing a queeny dance to 'Heatwave' by Martha Reeves and the Vandelles. Cut back to* GLENNDA *and* JUDY *laughing and have a grand old time).*

GLENNDA: I love this part.

JUDY: Me too, it's great.

(Together they catch themselves having too much fun, stop, turn around and shove their fork into the electric socket. Sparks fly as the pair are electrocuted).

GLENNDA: *(shaking violently)* This is just like *A Clockwork Lavender.*

JUDY: *(also shaking violently)* Yay!

GLENNDA: I'm actually enjoying this.

JUDY: It's kind of addictive.

GLENNDA: We can cure ourselves of our homosexuality and style our wigs at the same time.

(Their forks fly out of the socket and they go into a semi-coma. The Boys *video is still playing, the scene in which Harold [Leonard Frey] is reading Michael [Kenneth Williams] at the end of the film – Note: both actors, along with Robert LaTourneaux and Frederick Combs of the same film, have subsequently died of AIDS: 'You're a sad and pathetic man. You're a homosexual and you don't want to be. But there's nothing you can do to change it – not all your prayers to your god, not all the analysis you can buy in all the years you've got left to live. You may very well one day be able to know a heterosexual life – if you want it desperately enough. If you pursue it with the fervour with which you annihilate. But you'll always be homosexual as well. Always, Michael. Always. Until the day you*

die'. Cut to GLENNDA *and* JUDY *post-therapy, their wigs standing straight on end, trying to process their experience).*

GLENNDA and JUDY: (*together*) Woooa!

GLENNDA: Oh my god, Judy! That electro-shock therapy, it really worked!

JUDY: (*trying to tame her wig*) I like aversion therapy, it's fun.

GLENNDA: I feel like a new man.

JUDY: (*pushing her huge, unmanageable bangs from her face*) We should do it every day for twenty minutes.

GLENNDA: Yeah, it's our new workout. The XXX Gay Workout. So we're coming to the close of *Closet Talk*. We've covered a lot of territory . . .

JUDY: We forged a new Movement. . .

GLENNDA: . . .the *movement du jour* . . .

JUDY: . . . and I'd just like to say to all you youngsters out there who are thinking of coming out of the closet: There are other options. Think twice before coming out. Are you really cut out for a life in the theatre?

GLENNDA: There are modern precautions you can take to prevent all that. We live in the New Age. This is the future. We're arrived there, so there's new technology.

JUDY: Absolutely.

GLENNDA: Thanks for tuning in to *Closet Talk* . . .

JUDY: This is Judy LaBruce . . .

GLENNDA: . . . and Glennda Orgasm, signing off.

(The Closet Talk *theme song, 'Mongoloid' by Devo. Plays as the credits roll over a montage of the day's events;* GLENNDA *and* JUDY *with umbrellas mincing down Christopher Street, being whistled at by adoring passers-by, exiting a cab, being shocked, buzzing the buzzer at the Aesthetic Realist Foundation, and finally, spitting on the sidewalk in front of Stonewall).*